THE LORD OF THE RINGS
LOCATION GUIDEBOOK
EXTENDED EDITION

Ian Brodie

HarperCollins*Publishers*

The author and publisher wish to thank the following publications for their kind permission to use the quotations appearing on these pages: *Pavement Magazine* (pages 74, 75, 146 and 170); *The Lord of the Rings Official Movie Guide*, by Brian Sibley (pages 36, 51, 58, 118, 119, 166 and 169); the *Lord of the Rings Official Fan Club Magazine* (pages 155 and 172).

National Library of New Zealand Cataloguing-in-Publication Data

Brodie, Ian, 1957–
The Lord of the rings location guidebook / Ian Brodie.
Extended ed.
Previous ed.: 2003.
Includes index.
ISBN 1-86950-530-1
1. Motion picture locations—New Zealand—Guidebooks.
2. Lord of the rings, the fellowship of the ring (Motion picture)
3. Lord of the rings, the two towers (Motion picture)
4. Lord of the rings, the return of the king (Motion picture)
5. New Zealand—Guidebooks. I. Tolkien, J. R. R. (John Ronald Reuel),
1892–1973—Lord of the rings. II. Title.
919.30446dc 22

First published 2002
Revised Edition published 2003
This edition published 2004, reprinted 2004 (twice), 2005
HarperCollins*Publishers (New Zealand) Limited*
P.O. Box 1, Auckland

Front cover photo © New Line Productions; back cover photos: top four © Pierre Vinet/New Line Productions; bottom © Ian Brodie; page 8 © Chris Coad/New Line Productions

Designed by Gayna Murphy
Printed in China and produced by Phoenix Offset on 128gsm Matt Art

Acknowledgements

This book has only been possible through the help and support of many people and organisations. I would particularly like to thank Claire Raskind-Cooper — were it not for her support and enthusiasm the project would never have proceeded. Peter Jackson, Alan Lee, Viggo Mortensen, Jan Blenkin, Erin O'Donnell, Heather Patterson, Melissa Booth, Robin Murphy and all the other members of the LOTR cast and crew provided considerable help and suggestions, and Jane Dent and Anita Bhatnagar from Tourism New Zealand worked tirelessly to help the book reach fruition. Special thanks are also due to Producers Barrie M. Osborne and Fran Walsh.

Pierre Vinet

One of the many joys in completing this manuscript has been the totally enthusiastic people met on the road. Their local knowledge and expertise have helped me to understand the many and varied landscapes of New Zealand as well as allowing me to add many personal anecdotes within the pages. Thanks to Michael Stearne, Alfie Speight and Barbara Swan, John Von Tunzelman, Keith Falconer, Jill Herron, Russell and Dean Alexander, Hillary Finnie, 'Scottie', Paul Eames, Paul Lambert, Mike Mee, John Mahaffie, Chantel Ward, Simon and Priscilla Cameron, Matt Cooper, David McLaughlin, Mike Nolan, Tracey Dean and Bill Reid. My thanks also to the staff of all the Regional Tourism Organisations in New Zealand I pestered for information, who were so quick to offer their help.

The use of modern technology has allowed this book to be compiled 'on the fly' in some unusual locations. Thanks to Anton Napier (Philips), Bryan Morton (Computerland), Ken Goody (Kodak) for photographic support, Thomas Electronics (GPS) and Topo Map World (Electronic Maps).

Thanks also to Brian Sibley, author of the *Official Movie Guide*, and Bernard McDonald, Editor of *Pavement Magazine*, for their kind permission to use quotes from their interviews with the cast and crew.

My wife, Dianne, and children, Travis and Sally-Anne, have coped with months of *The Lord of the Rings* — thanks. Jane Johnson, Lorain Day and Sue Page at HarperCollins*Publishers* have calmly coped with my many queries and requests for information, and Chris Winitana wrote a superb introduction.

This book is dedicated to J.R.R. Tolkien for his vision and Peter Jackson for making this vision three-dimensional.

Ian Brodie
Wanaka 2004

Foreword

Pierre Vinet

Eighteen years old and reading J.R.R. Tolkien for the first time, I was sitting on a train as it left Wellington and rumbled up through the North Island. During the twelve-hour journey, I'd lift my eyes from the book and look at the familiar landscape — which all of a sudden looked like Middle-earth. That was over twenty years ago. Since then this story has ceased to exist for me as a work of fiction, instead it has become an account of an extraordinary passage of time. Tolkien's Middle-earth is based on a detailed mythical prehistory of this planet as it was about 6000 or 7000 years ago. For me, it reads more like history than fantasy, a fully developed society and environment the records have since forgotten.

Bringing that world to life has been a fantastic and incredibly difficult journey, but one made special because of the people and places of New Zealand. There was never any question the film wouldn't be made here. With the variety of landscapes of such an awesome nature, and the opportunity to involve talented Kiwis in a major production, it was the only way to go.

After three years of planning, on 11 October 1999, myself and a dedicated cast and crew of over 2500 people began our cinematic journey. We wanted the Middle-earth the viewer saw to feel believable and it was fantastic having Tolkien's richly created world to research all the detail. I went back and re-read particular scenes to get the image right before we started filming.

The Waikato farming country where we created Hobbiton was a like a slice of ancient England. I knew Hobbiton needed to be warm, comfortable and feel lived in. By letting the weeds grow through the cracks and establishing hedges and little gardens a year before filming, we ended up with an incredibly real place, not just a film set. It felt as if you could open the circular green door of Bag End and find Bilbo Baggins inside. Whakapapa Ski Field's rocky escarpment was the complete opposite. From one extreme to another — here the barren and inhospitable landscape was already the perfect embodiment of Mordor.

Tolkien's world was one of deep hidden valleys, barren wastelands, remote mystical mountains and lush, low valleys, and we found all these places throughout New Zealand. Many were only accessible by helicopter and getting crew in and out wasn't easy. On reflection, I can see it had a hidden benefit — the hardships imposed by difficult country and challenging weather probably gave the actors and crew a strong sense of the reality of the characters' journey through Middle-earth. We took risks with the weather, shooting in extreme environments, such as Mt Ruapehu, Lake

Mavora, Kaitoke Regional Park, Mt Cook and Mt Olympus — the landscape and raw beauty of these places were ideal for the story.

Standing at any of the 100 locations, watching Tolkien's characters come to life before my eyes, has been one of the real pleasures of my experience as director, writer and producer. The opportunity to helm a project of this size, scope and grandeur has been a once-in-a-lifetime experience, something that eighteen-year-old on the train never imagined.

Most of the crew were new to this kind of project. Their hard work and enthusiasm, combined with fantastic locations and computer enhancement technology all came together in a special way which gives our movies a unique feel — different from the Hollywood blockbusters we're used to seeing. With the help of this guidebook Tolkien fans, for whom the films were made, can experience their own unique insight into the magic and complexity of Middle-earth, and the adventure we had in order to bring it to life. My only gripe is that this book didn't exist when we started — it would have saved a huge amount of location hunting!

Peter Jackson

Contents

Ian Brodie

Ian Brodie

Travis Brodie

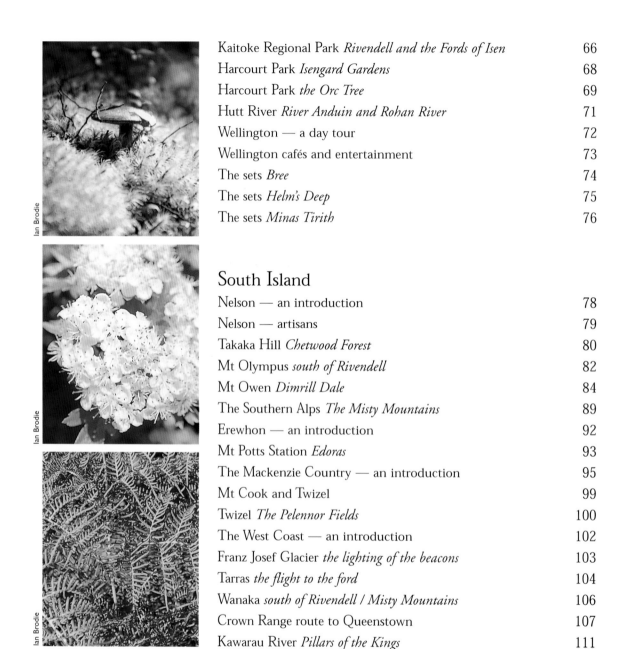

Ian Brodie

Ian Brodie

Ian Brodie

South Island

Ian Brodie

Ian Brodie

Ian Brodie

Ian Brodie

Ian Brodie

Travis Brodie

Introduction to New Zealand's mythology

Before the beginning there alone was Io, Io-the-parentless, Io-the-endless, Io-the-timeless, Io-without-limit.

He moved and the Great Nothingness was born. In the spiralling currents it followed itself and searched. It found heart and became ignited. It thought as does a mind. And desired as does a dream. It took form and breathed. And in a second that was a million years, it multiplied and grew. To become a shadow. A darkness. A night. A night of gestation. A night for bearing the Ancients.

There was Ranginui, the virile male, sky-bound and active. There was Papatuanuku, the female, land-bound and passive. They breathed together as lovers and in the Night-that-knows-no-end there were born to them seventy mighty sons. There was Whiro-the-dominant whose wrath was as an axe upon the tree, and Tawhiri-of-the-elements, whose breath was the wind itself. There was Tangaroa-of-the-seas, whose ceaseless waves would chisel away the land. There was Tu-of-the-red-face, by whose hand mankind would know war, and Turongo-the-gentle who would lay down the foundations of peace. There was Haumia-the-abundant who was lord over the fruits of the earth and Ruaumoko-the-lastborn, whose one tiny movement would cause the earth herself to quake and tremor. Finally there was Tane-the-thoughtful, whose actions and deeds would produce the world and all its parts.

It was Tane who separated their parents to produce the sky above and the land below. And when his grieving parents' tears filled the world, he turned his mother over to stop Ranginui from having to look upon her face and be reminded of their separation.

Tane brought light to the world by placing the stars in the sky, the sun at its zenith and the moon lower down on his father's head. He built the first house of nobility and it remains to this day the blueprint from which all homes are templated. He filled it with the knowledge of the gods, which he retrieved from the summit of the heavens at the instruction of Io-the-creator himself. He produced the trees, the birds, the insects and fish to clothe and adorn his mother, the earth. Finally, he created the first human, a woman from whom all peoples are descended. The world of eternal light where all beings were kin, no matter who or what, was born.

Many times did summer and winter struggle in rivalry before Maui-of-the-topknot, half-man, half-god, was gifted to the world. Raised by his priestly elder, Tamanui, he was shown the secrets of the universe; the kinship that existed between all things that would allow him to take on the form of the tree, the bird, the fish, the lizard. He mastered himself and returned to his family ready to conquer.

With a fearless heart he secured the magic jawbone of knowledge of his ancestress Murirangawhenua. And with it he caught and slowed down the sun, which sped across the heavens at will with little thought for the activities of man. He made fire available to people by forcing the very last flame of the Keeper-of-the-fires, Mahuika, to become imbued into the heartwood of the tree. He visited the spirit world to find his father and before his death at the hands of the Goddess-of-death, Hine-nui-te-po, he fished up these sacred isles.

Using the sacred jawbone as a hook, Maui-the-relentless hauled up his great fish from the depths of Te Moananui a Kiwa, the Pacific Ocean. But as he paid homage to the gods for having given him such a wondrous gift, with greed in their eyes and lies on their tongues his four brothers took to the fish with knives. In its death throes it became torn and shredded with gullies and gorges, hills and mountains. In time, the stingray-like fish became the North Island of New Zealand while the canoe of Maui became the South Island.

The head of the fish is at our capital city, Wellington. The ridge of mountain ranges that run down the centre of the island is its backbone. To the east coast and west to Taranaki can be seen its fins. The stomach is Lake Taupo while the heart is at Maunga Pohatu in the Ureweras. Northland is the whipping tail of the stingray. From tip to tip, fish to canoe, can be seen the myriad of extremities of this once virgin land.

And many centuries ago, when the voyager Kupe with his family and wife came upon these islands shrouded in mist and cloud they named them Aotearoa, land of the long white cloud.

Chris Winitana

The location hunting process

The way the location process works is that generally a location scout goes out in advance and canvasses the whole country for potential places. We made up a list of what we needed, which obviously came from the book because Tolkien describes the locations very vividly in *The Lord of the Rings*. You can just imagine them in your mind's eye so it was pretty mandatory for the location scouts to read the book.

Dave Comer, Robin Murphy and various other people scoured New Zealand and sent me photographs and videotapes. It was almost like casting for an actor, and the process is really the same, with somebody doing the initial sweep and then once we narrow down the choices, and we see places we'd like, we go out for what's called a 'recce'.

This was a team of people including myself, Andrew Lesnie, our Director of Photography, Caro Cunningham, the First Assistant Director, and a whole slew of technical support people. We would look at the landscape from an artistic point of view, first of all to see if it was suitable and does this feel like it came from the pages of Tolkien's book? Then you look at it from a logistical point of view, because the second consideration is where do we park the trucks?

Where can we feed the crew? Is there a road in here — and sometime there wasn't — but that didn't necessarily stop us! So while there were a whole lot of considerations, first and foremost the question was always 'is this like it was described in the book?'

Top: Peter Jackson
relaxes at Whakapapa.

Above: Caro
Cunningham on location.

15

Pierre Vinet

Taking in that wonderful remote landscape at Poolburn.

I think my favourite locations were the helicopter-access only ones, locations that don't have roads or tracks. Norwest Lakes near Te Anau was my absolute favourite. We shot some scenes from a helicopter of the Fellowship heading towards *Moria*. There are only two or three shots in the movie, but they are very special to me.

Just to land there, and get out of the helicopter and walk around is fantastic, it's an amazingly stunning place. Beautiful land. Mount Olympus and Mount Owen are also two places I would never have gone normally because I'm not a tramper. The fact that because we've made these movies, I've got to see these incredibly magical remote places, is something I'm really grateful for.

Another place I loved was Poolburn in Central Otago. We were looking for the nation of *Rohan* and in the book Tolkien describes these grasslands pretty much like the Steppes of Russia, or the prairie lands of America with grass as far as the eye can see. We don't really have anything quite like that in New Zealand. We do, however, have this place in Central Otago near Poolburn, which has an enormous expanse of slightly undulating hills with these really jagged rocks. They are definitely not described by Tolkien, but none the less, it did look like a dramatic and amazing landscape.

It also had a sense of scale. Whenever you can put a camera down, and literally see 50 km in one direction, and have no power poles, no houses, no roads, it's just expanse, it suddenly gives the film that kind of epic John Ford western quality of tiny figures in this big landscape. So Poolburn really fitted the bill perfectly for us as *Rohan* because it had the scale of landscape we needed.

It was an interesting little place, a little tiny settlement with little weekend holiday homes near the shores of the lake. I found the whole place to be very, very fascinating and of all the locations we went to, it's my other favourite.

Peter Jackson

Cameras in Middle-earth

Peter Jackson loves to keep the camera active and very wild, keeping an incredible amount of energy in the shots, as ultimately, the world is never seen from a stagnant perspective in our own reality. So on film, Peter loves to keep this very organic and gritty feeling. Watching the different technicians on location, there was such a level of ingenuity brought to the day's work, but I thought that of any department, the people who really brought special skills to what Peter required were the camera department — the grips and the camera operators. They invented equipment, in the middle of nowhere, that could achieve the sort of shots Peter imagined. You have these massive, sweeping landscapes with these energetic shots flying around inside the forests or across lakes, and Harry Harrison and his team of grips would invent this equipment on the day to do these wonderful ideas that were popping up in Peter's head.

A steady-cam captures the action at Paradise.

The thing I loved watching more than anything else while we were filming *The Lord Of The Rings* was the flying fox camera. At Paradise, near Glenorchy, there is this massive forest where we filmed the Uruk-hai surging down the hill as this mighty force chasing the poor Hobbits. Peter wanted the camera to feel like it was your point of view so the camera department built this incredible system through the treetops, where they found a direct journey, and put these massive cables that went hundreds of feet through the forest. They then suspended this huge camera off it and flew it through the trees. It created some hysterical rushes that night, because the poor Uruk-hai are madly running as fast as they can, unaware of where the camera is in relationship to them. On two occasions, the camera came sweeping down a little bit too close to these poor, hapless Uruk-hai, clipped them and sent them flying off. They ended up unhurt, thankfully, but it made for some hysterical filming.

Pierre Vinet

My favourite location would have to be *Edoras*. There was no place in my life I have been to that more succinctly captured a culture than Mt Potts. It also realised, for me, the vision of the written word, and ultimately, the art that was generated around *The Lord Of The Rings*. To walk through this village, completely fabricated as a set, but on a mountain, on this huge, craggy piece of rock with a 360-degree panoramic view of these massive, sweeping mountains covered in snow with the plains down below was an absolute treat. Then the art department had the audacity and the vision to build an amazing city on top of this huge, rocky outcrop.

To enter *Edoras* on the days I was blessed to work there, and stand amongst the villagers and the royal guards of *Rohan*, near *King Theoden* and *Éowyn*, and be a part of the crew in this magical environment, transported me well beyond standing amongst ruins in an ancient city around the world, or in the midst of a cathedral in Britain.

I stood in another world — one created by a bunch of New Zealanders on the top of a mountain in the middle of nowhere, and it felt utterly real.

Richard Taylor

Middle-earth in New Zealand

The landscapes of Middle-earth were forged in Tolkien's imagination from a combination of memories of places he'd known and the mythical lands he encountered during his studies of ancient texts. His descriptions of the *Shire*, the *Misty Mountains* and the golden woods of *Lothlórien* are evocative enough to make these places seem tangible, but we each bring our own memories and dreams into play when we imagine them. While his love of England may have been the foundation stone of Middle-earth, we didn't believe we would find there, or anywhere else in Europe, a landscape that was not so steeped in its own history that it could serve as the background for his epic. As a result, I found the prospect of looking for Middle-earth in a country reminiscent of Europe but lacking the accumulated and overlaid evidence of thousands of years of continual habitation intriguing.

We travelled widely to far-flung parts of the country, led by our location scout, Dave Comer, looking for the perfect *Hobbiton*, *Rivendell* and *Bree*, finding a lovely location for *Hobbiton*, with hills that looked as though Hobbits had already begun excavations. It had a lake with a long arm we could pass off as a river, the perfect spot for a bridge, a mill and *'The Green Dragon'*, a *Party Tree* and an ideal situation for *Bag End*. It only needed an ancient tree, which our Greens Department, under Brian Massey, constructed and painstakingly foliated with plastic leaves. After several months of earth moving, set building, hedge laying and gardening the place felt as though it had been inhabited by generations of Hobbits, and it was satisfying to see it had taken on something of the look of the Devonshire countryside I'd lived in for the past twenty-five years.

As we wanted a less benign and cultivated look for the countryside around *Bree* we ended up close to Wellington, where we used land owned by the military on the Miramar peninsula for the outskirts, while the *Prancing Pony* and surrounding streets were built around barracks at Fort Dorset, in Seatoun.

Above top: An incongruous combination. Light refreshments are undertaken on the 'slopes' of Caradhras.

Above: Easterlings prepare for battle in Wellington.

Above: Aragorn
and Éowyn rehearse
lines — Deer Park
Heights.

Opposite above:
The Dead Marshes.
Alan Lee

Opposite below:
Rivendell scene
at Kaitoke
Regional Park.
Alan Lee

Mount Ruapehu was an obvious first stop in the search for *Mordor* and the site of the battle on the slopes of *Mount Doom*, with the prologue for *The Fellowship of the Ring* shot in the off-season ski field at Whakapapa. *Frodo* and *Sam* tramped back and forth over a nearby area Peter liked the look of for the *Emyn Muil* — the vast labyrinth of rocks our heroes have to find their way through on their journey to the *Black Gates*, and where they first meet *Gollum*.

The *Weathertop* scenes were shot on a station at Port Waikato, where strangely shaped limestone outcrops and disfigured trees in a green landscape wouldn't have been out of place in the background of an Hieronymus Bosch painting. We found the perfect hill for the *Ringwraiths'* attack, with the ruins of *Amon Sûl* built in a studio and the wider views established in a matte painting.

We visited Skippers Canyon several times looking for the ford where *Arwen* and *Frodo* face the *Ringwraiths*, and the digitally created flood you see in the finished movie was only slightly more impressive than the real one that swept away one of our sets after a particularly heavy rainfall! I'm always looking for interesting rock formations and textures, which I use to ensure the 'bones' of any of my pictures also have a story to tell, and so that the rocks and stones I draw don't always look the same. Skippers Canyon provided some great material, and also formed a suitably grand setting for the Fellowship's journey down the *Anduin*, and for the *Argonath*.

Our search for *Rivendell* took us far and wide, but although we found useful elements, we never found one place with everything we wanted. We eventually chose Kaitoke because of its beautiful, calm woodlands and proximity to Wellington, but its surroundings in the film are a combination of filmed elements such as waterfalls, photographs, paintings and a miniature built at Weta Workshop, long before we knew where we would be filming.

Paradise, near Glenorchy at the northern end of Lake Wakatipu, worked well for parts of *Lothlórien*, though we added larger trees, and for scenes at *Parth Galen* and *Amon Hen*. I loved the landscape around Poolburn, where many of the *Rohan* scenes were shot, with its rolling hills and dramatic granite tors reminding me of Dartmoor, although on a much grander scale. Mount Potts, near Methven, provided one of the most glorious locations, with an isolated hill in a wide valley, buttressed by sheer cliffs, which couldn't have been closer to Tolkien's *Edoras*. We built the exterior of the

Alan Lee

Pierre Vinet

Golden Hall and surrounding buildings on top with the gatehouse and more buildings at its foot, with everything in between added post-production.

We were always on the lookout for wetland areas for the *Dead Marshes* between the *Emyn Muil* and the *Black Gates*. In the end all the scenes were shot on sets created by our Greens Department, with wider views shot from helicopters. Once we'd landed, we quickly realised the impracticality of filming in a place where we'd have to count the crew after each take.

Above top: Mountain storms in the Wizard's Vale, near Glenorchy.

Above: Deer Park Heights near Queenstown provided a very useful location for filming. The Riders of Rohan stand tall above the civilisation below.

I found New Zealand more than matched my hopes as a setting for *The Lord of the Rings*. It has such a wide variety of landscapes, from lush farmland, woods and rivers to dramatic gorges, endless plains and soaring mountains uninterrupted by roads and pylons. It's a young land, primeval in places, still flexing in the aftermath of its creation. I can imagine Britain in a much earlier age, with higher peaks and the clearer light that illuminates Tolkien's pages, might have had a similar quality.

It has been a pleasure, and a privilege, to have seen so much of New Zealand's rich and beautiful landscapes with guides whose wealth of experience was matched only by their love of their country and enthusiasm for our journey.

Alan Lee
Conceptual Artist/Set Decorator

Finding the locations

I knew what was in store as I was completing production in Sydney on *The Matrix* and headed for Wellington. I'd filmed in New Zealand before and looked forward to rekindling friendships and meeting film-makers Peter Jackson and Fran Walsh to discuss the possibility of producing *The Lord of the Rings* as part of their team.

We talked over a hearty lunch, dining seaside at The Chocolate Fish Café. It was a sunny afternoon on Wellington's southern coast, with a family atmosphere, convivial and comfortable. It felt creative, cohesive and challenging. I couldn't think of a better place to mount the mammoth movie trilogy, *The Lord of the Rings,* nor could I imagine passing up the opportunity to work with such an innovative director as Peter Jackson.

Pierre Vinet

At Amon Hen (Closeburn) with beautiful Lake Wakatipu in the background.

Filming three films at once is unprecedented, an effort not to be undertaken lightly. It's hard enough to wrap one film on time, let alone three, and is a great testament to the dedication, motivation and talent of the cast, crew and film-making team.

The landscapes of J.R.R. Tolkien's Middle-earth are all here in New Zealand. We scouted locations in the North and South Islands by car, by helicopter, on foot, and by boat. We began armed with the detailed descriptive passages in Tolkien's novels, then we were guided by the illustrations produced through Peter Jackson's collaboration with conceptual artists Alan Lee and John Howe, searching for places that mirrored the unique details of their drawings. They are truly amazing.

I remember a short flight to the South Island. From the time we took off, to the time we landed, Alan sketched several illustrations showing how a proposed set would fit into the landscape. I also remember scouting *Rivendell*, walking about at Kaitoke planning how we would get our equipment into the location, figuring where sets might go and action be staged. Meanwhile, Alan and John sat quietly on a hillside producing illustrations siting the various set elements in the very landscape we were scouting.

To translate *The Lord of the Rings* from novel to screen we wanted the texture of the trilogy to stand out as something that captured the unique land of Middle-earth.

Filming the Oliphant scene at Twelve Mile Delta.

From the outset Peter and I pledged to shoot in the best location rather than the easiest. Mount Potts, which is *Edoras* in *The Two Towers*, is evidence of going that extra mile. Without that commitment, we might have easily, but unfortunately, shot the entire film on a back lot or a green screen stage instead of in the wonderful settings of New Zealand.

As a film-maker, it's important to honor your financial commitment to the studio but at the same time, not be blinkered by a dollars and cents mentality. Although the bottom line is always an important factor, you equally must find the funds to shoot the essential elements of your script. On *The Lord of the Rings*, one of those elements is the breathtakingly stunning New Zealand locations. If you need to build a road to get to that isolated mountaintop at Mount Potts, you build the road. You owe it to a project like *The Lord of the Rings* to secure that raw, untouched beauty and vision on film. It certainly paid off in the appeal of the films and therefore at the box office.

Pierre Vinet

No matter how specific a location Peter Jackson imagined, our locations department never came up empty-handed. There was always that isolated mountaintop, lush forest, crystal clear lake, or eerie desert just waiting to be discovered. Sometimes it felt like these remote places were just waiting to double as Tolkien's Middle-earth. Tolkien's descriptions were right there in front of us in their three-dimensional glory waiting to grace the camera with their natural beauty. I find it hard to believe that Alan Lee and John Howe didn't hike out to Mount Potts to sketch the illustration for *Edoras* or wander into Matamata to find the inspiration for *Gandalf* arriving at *Bag End*.

Our production logistics were difficult. Over one hundred locations and three hundred sets were spread all over the country. It wasn't unusual on any given shooting day to have three, four, or even five different crews filming simultaneously.

The Kiwi film crew's dedication was unparalleled in my experience of producing

Pierre Vinet

Above top: Part of the huge set construction of Minas Tirith.

Above: Standing amidst the splendid isolation of Twizel.

Above; Camera being prepared at Twizel.

Right: Filming the Riders of Rohan at Poolburn.

movies. They never complained about the long hours on set or the adverse weather we frequently filmed in, treating their work with great pride. Their ingenuity is celebrated in every frame of the film. I've never been part of anything compared to this size, scope, and grandeur, and doubt I ever will be again.

We also explored the country during our time off. We compared stories of fly fishing, bungy jumping, skiing, sailing, tramping, and just about every other outdoor activity you can think of.

I will always treasure my time in New Zealand, as I continue to make films throughout the world. Where else in the world can you have such natural beauty combined with a commute to work where you don't hit one traffic light, and during those long summer days there is a stunning sunrise right outside your window?

Even though I'm American by birth, for the rest of my days, when I return to New Zealand, I imagine I will always take one breath of the fresh air on arrival and feel as if I have come home.

Barrie M. Osborne

A day in the life of an extra

In June 2003 Director Peter Jackson graciously allowed my 15-year-old son Travis and I to spend three weeks on set during pick-up filming for *The Return of the King*. As well as being able to meet many of the cast and crew we both obtained small parts as extras in the film. We were like kids in a candy shop.

A clock-radio alarm sounding in your hotel room at 4 00 a.m. normally means the settings are wrong, but for Travis and I this alarm was the opening sound for a day that would allow us to become part of cinematic history. Arriving at the Stone St Studios at 4 45 a.m. to a hive of activity and bustle was unexpected — what time do the workers start?

For Travis the first stop is clothing — rags that would befit an orc of the army of Sauron marching from Minas Ithil to wage war on Gondor. These orcs are regimented and must be able to march correctly so the team is then assembled and an ex New Zealand Army Drill Sergeant spends an hour teaching them to march in unison.

Next is a visit to the Weta workers who splash mud with a brush onto the clothes before finding armour and then fitting the grotesque head. This is then conveniently placed in a carry bag for later use. An army marches on its stomach so breakfast is important — all cooked to order by Flying Trestles. It's funny in the catering tent, with the orcs all sitting together ravenously devouring all the food in sight while the Gondorians and Rohirrim are in separate corners — there will be no fraternisation with the enemy, even over breakfast.

Then the waiting commences — it's only 7 00 a.m. but all is ready. By 9 00 a.m. the call is made to Stage Q. From the outside we look at an old warehouse but walking in the door we are transported to a rocky path leading down through the desolation of Mordor. Two days earlier on the same stage Travis and I watched Theoden King rally his troops at Dunharrow in preparation for the Ride of the Rohirrim.

A crew of hundreds are fussing with cameras, recorders, dollies and props, with Weta workers on hand to ensure all orcish features are correct. The cast are assembled on stage, torches are lit, cameras are rolling, the crew disappear from sight and the buzzer sounds. 'Shooting!' The orcs march for twenty seconds. 'Cut!' Like a wave, the crew return, retouching make-up, checking props and when all is ready again the wave retreats.

After an hour of this, morning tea is served. Hobbits must love their parts in these films — this was a second breakfast rather than a snack. Heads are removed and orcs

Travis Brodie

Dianne Brodie

The author as a Rohirrim soldier and Gondorian bread seller.

Ian Brodie

Travis Brodie

**GENETIC DEPT
THREE FOOT SIX LTD
MIRAMAR WGTN**

Top: Orc marching
practice.

Above: A sense of
humour on one of
the transportation
trucks.

from all walks of life discuss the day's happenings over bacon and coffee.

The day wears on but there's no further shooting until after lunch. Another scene is shot and then all remains quiet until 5 00 p.m. It's twelve hours since our arrival and 45 minutes of work has been spread over the day. Who cares! All we have to do now is wait six months to see if the orc march has made the grade.

My part in this epic commenced two months before shooting. 'If you want to be a soldier of Rohan or a civilian in Minas Tirith you need a beard,' I was told. No problems — I'd grow an extra finger if I thought it was going to get me into the movie. Arriving in Wellington my first visit is to casting. I am to be part of the celebrations at Edoras following the Battle of Helms Deep. Report tomorrow at 5 30 a.m. Today the early morning buzzer means I will be transported into Middle-earth. Clothing is fitted and breakfast is served but it appears this isn't to be the opening scene of my new acting career. No wig can be found to fit.

Disappointed, I return to the Age of Men and sit on the sidelines, watching

Theoden, Eowyn and Aragorn discuss their fortunes. My disappointment disappears very quickly as I sit on stage watching Peter direct and then afterwards discuss the *Location GuideBook* with Bernard, Miranda and Viggo. I pinch myself — is this really happening?

Two days later I'm back at casting. I'm to be a Gondorian market seller. A wig and clothing are fitted and a Polaroid is taken for continuity.

Over the last few weeks I've watched the streets of Minas Tirith come to life from wood and polystyrene. Now they are completed and the realisation that I will soon be working on them causes a huge surge of excitement.

The drive through the darkened streets of a midwinter morning in Wellington, to the hive of activity at Miramar, is now very familiar. In wardrobe my costume is fitted and then an hour is spent as the grey locks of a wig are fitted over my own grey hair. As I look in the mirror the transformation is remarkable.

By 10 30 a.m. I am comfortably through second breakfast and have acquainted myself with my fellow artistes. All is ready as we are ushered to the outside set. The crew arrive with their amazing portable units. Screens, tables and a comfortable chair for Peter, a computer and office on a trolley for Barrie, other wheeled units for sound and continuity. What had been a deserted set only an hour ago is now filled with that amazing wave of people preparing for action. The set is dressed down to the smallest degree and I practice my part of selling bread to other civilians who are still left in this city under siege.

All at once Peter arrives and Sir Ian takes his place next to me! Gandalf has sent Pippin to light the beacons and as he stands on the street he watches gleefully as the first fire is lit. I sell bread.

Peter directs the scene, which is shot about six times from various angles and then he is happy and Gandalf is happy in the knowledge that the Riders of Rohan will soon be on their way. I change back into jeans and wander over for lunch. Ten minutes of action in a day to remember.

Six months later I settle into a theatre seat for the culmination of two years of movie magic. The film is wonderful and what makes it more exciting are the scene of the orcs marching (with a shorter one in the front) and the view of half a grey head next to Gandalf in Minas Tirith.

Ian Brodie

Ian Brodie

Ian Brodie

Previous page: Travis
is transformed
into an orc.

Above: Shooting the
scene on the road
leaving Minas Ithil.

Right: The author
at Minas Tirith
without a wig.

Ian Brodie

Port Waikato *Weathertop*

The ancient watchtower of *Weathertop* where *Frodo* was attacked by the *Black Riders* is a combination of real countryside and studio set. Although the scenes showing *Aragorn* leading the Hobbits to the base of the hill were filmed on private land, very similar landscapes can be viewed near Port Waikato, a two-hour drive from Auckland.

Ian Brodie

Spectacular views of the Weather Hills south of Port Waikato.

To reach *Amon Sûl* travel initially out of Auckland on the Southern Motorway to Pukekohe, a town surrounded by fertile ground yielding some of the best potatoes and vegetables in New Zealand. Drive on to Tuakau before crossing the mighty Waikato River (New Zealand's longest river) and continue a further 30 km to the small seaside hamlet of Port Waikato. Here the Waikato River finally reaches the sea, after a journey of more than 350 km from Lake Taupo in the centre of the North Island. Port Waikato is a popular holiday retreat for many Aucklanders who escape from the city to enjoy a break of swimming and fishing.

Leaving the holiday homes behind, continue south on the only road heading south (unpaved) for approximately 10 km and you will enter a landscape very reminiscent of the *Weather Hills of Eregion*. The road winds through a lush valley of grass and streams whilst all around the hills frown down upon you, with the most incredible limestone faces and bluffs. There are many places here to stop for a picnic lunch and savour this very Middle-earth landscape.

Note that if you are planning to travel to *Hobbiton*, it is possible to continue on this road to Hamilton and then on to Matamata. Allow 3 hours.

Amon Sûl (Sindarin 'The Hill of Winds') was a watchtower built on Weathertop Hill by Elendil in the Third Age. A palantír was held here until 1409 (TA) when the tower was attacked by a huge army led by the Witch-king of Angmar. The palantír was carried to safety but the tower was forsaken and fell into ruins.

Matamata *Hobbiton*

Pierre Vinet

Ian Brodie

Above top: Sam Gamgee and Frodo leaving the Shire.

Above: A signpost at Hobbiton.

The Waikato region of the North Island is one of the richest farming areas in New Zealand. Driving south on State Highway One, the urban sprawl of Auckland is soon replaced by paddocks and hedgerows.

A district of rolling grassy hills, Matamata is a small part of England transported to the other side of the world. The name means point or headland in Maori, and the area was named after Te Waharoa Pa, which jutted out into a swamp, rendering it impregnable.

The area's development can be accredited to an Englishman, Josiah Clifton Firth, who emigrated from Yorkshire in 1855. Travelling south on business, he established a lasting friendship with local Maori and by 1884 had purchased 56,000 acres of swampy marshland. With a strong vision for the area, he commenced large-scale drainage of the fens and planted vast paddocks in grass, barley, wheat and oats. In the ensuing years the area was transformed as hedgerows grew alongside oaks and elms and the area prospered as the railway probed south from Auckland. Today Matamata remains a country service town, but Matamata's rich grassland now produces another lucrative crop; the Waikato has developed into New Zealand's main racehorse-breeding area.

There are two routes to this town of wide streets and friendly faces — turn off before Pokeno and travel on SH27, or continue on SH1 through Hamilton and turn left towards Piarere.

Venture south of Matamata on Hinuera Road (SH27) and it soon becomes apparent why *Hobbiton* was created here, thousands of kilometres from Sarehole and Tolkien's rural England; the hedgerow-lined lanes provide glimpses of paddocks and grassy downs that are a vision of the *Shire*.

Pause at Piarere — the strange rock formations reveal this whole valley was once a

Alan Lee

Pierre Vinet

Above: Hobbiton in the peaceful Shire.

Left: Gandalf the Grey greets Bilbo at Bag End.

Ian Brodie

riverbed, with rocky escarpments left stranded high on the sides of hills that once channelled water. Known as the Hinuera Formation, these rocks are a set of alluvial sands, gravels and silts deposited in the basin during the period of the Last Glaciation (between 50,000 and 15,000 years ago). In 1999, these peaceful paddocks were transformed into the *Green Hill Country* of the *Shire, Middle-earth*.

Guided tours to *Hobbiton* operate daily (no private visits are allowed). The two hour excursion must be booked at the Matamata Visitor Information Centre. Entry into Middle-earth begins when you board your mini-van, as your guide explains how part of the Alexander's sheep farm was transformed into the *Shire*. You will be driven along a road specifically built by the New Zealand Army to allow access to *Hobbiton* and as you climb the brow of a hill, suddenly the set is directly ahead.

On a stroll around *Hobbiton* your guide will explain how the set developed, with plenty of opportunities for photographs. Conveniently situated photo boards show how the area looked during filming and the work required by talented set designers to achieve the amazing finished look. The culmination of the tour is a walk up *Bagshot Row* to *Bag End*, to stand outside the most famous Hobbit hole in Middle-earth.

Returning to town, the Workman's Café in the main street is a local icon. With its eccentric décor and slightly eccentric staff, it makes a welcome stop for lunch or dinner.

Anyone with an interest in thoroughbred horses should take an early drive to the local racecourse and see over 500 horses being taken for their morning exercise as the sun rises over the horizon.

Above: Hobbit holes around The Hill.

Opposite above: Bagshot Row, as seen in The Fellowship of the Ring. Alan Lee

Opposite below: Imported hedgerows and trees still flourish at Hobbiton. Ian Brodie

INTERNET
www.waikatonz.co.nz
www.hobbitontours.com

Central North Island locations

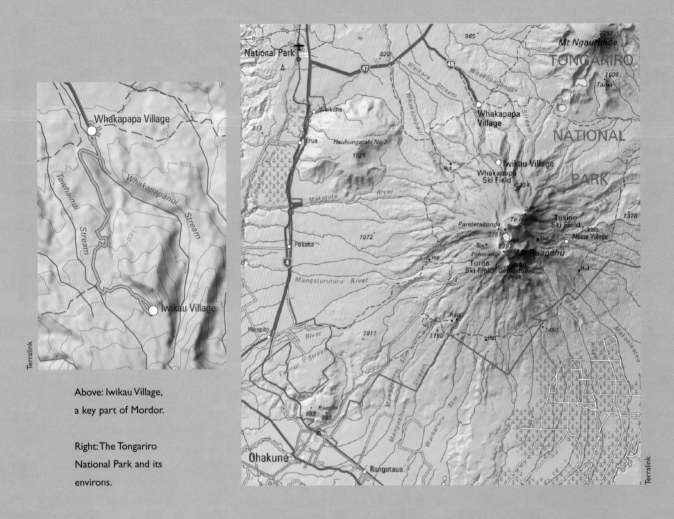

Above: Iwikau Village, a key part of Mordor.

Right: The Tongariro National Park and its environs.

New Zealand is gorgeous! I don't really think that there's anywhere else we could have filmed this movie unless we had travelled to lots of different places around the world. Every element of Middle-earth is contained in New Zealand. It's perfect. There are so many different geographical landscapes: mountains, woods, marshes, desert areas, rolling hills — and the sea. Everything, in fact, described in The Lord of the Rings. ELIJAH WOOD

The Central North Island is an area of distinctive geography and contrasting scenery. In the space of an hour you can travel from a peaceful wonderland of rivers, lakes and pastoral greenery to a blasted, tormented landscape of lava and volcanic ash.

This area was once one of the most prolific volcanic areas in the world, with Lake Taupo formed as a result of the largest eruption seen in the last 5000 years. The Oruanui Eruption, 26,500 years ago, created the shape of the lake, then in 181 AD a further explosion produced an eruption column 50 km high with over 30 km of pumice, ash and rock fragments ejected in minutes. The effects of the eruption were seen in the sky as far away as Europe and China.

Sitting beside New Zealand's largest lake (619 km²) Taupo serves as an ideal base for visiting all areas of the volcanic plateau, including the thermal resort of Rotorua, the world-famous fishing area of the Tongariro River or the mountainous region of Tongariro National Park.

Home to a kaleidoscope of bubbling mud, geysers and pristine lakes, the thermal wonderland of Rotorua is a one-hour drive to the north and one of the most popular tourist destinations in New Zealand.

South of Taupo is Tongariro National Park, New Zealand's first national park and a world heritage area. The park was created in 1887 when three volcanoes, Ruapehu, Ngauruhoe and Tongariro, were gifted to the people of New Zealand by Ngati Tuwharetoa, the local iwi.

Viggo Mortensen

Above: Taupo (2000) by Viggo Mortensen.

Below: Lake Taupo, a boatie's paradise. Nearby, the Ariatiatia Rapids on the Waikato River were used as a reference for the flooding of Isengard.

Destination Lake Taupo

INTERNET

www.laketauponz.co.nz

37

Tongariro National Park *Mordor*

New Line Productions

Ian Brodie

Above top: Frodo and Sam in the Emyn Muil.

Above: Now abseilers use the same place.

Opposite: Tawhai Falls near the Grand Chateau.

Ian Brodie

The drive from Taupo to the Grand Chateau follows SH1 around Lake Taupo to Turangi, a good stop for anglers wishing to fish the world-famous Tongariro River. A licence, obtained from information centres and local Department of Conservation (DOC) offices, is required to fish New Zealand lakes, and it would be wise to check on the local fishing season.

At Rangipo turn right onto SH46 and after 41 km turn left onto SH48 — the Grand Chateau is a further 10 km on. Pause at Tawhai Falls, 4 km up this road and take the twenty-minute walk which will give you a view of the falls, which are well worth a visit. The beech and toatoa-lined river tumbling over an ancient lava flow into a rock pool can easily be imagined as *Henneth Annûn*.

The Grand Chateau, one of the most iconic hotels in New Zealand, sits in splendid isolation at the foot of Mt Ruapehu in Tongariro National Park. Just one hour's drive south from Taupo, the hotel was built in the 1920s and features huge floor to ceiling windows to make the most of the outstanding views.

The *Lord of the Rings* team stayed here for a number of weeks, using the conference room as their headquarters and the cinema to view the film 'rushes'. The great advantage of staying at this hotel, of course, is the ability to drive 15 minutes and be transported into the heart of *Mordor*.

The highest peak in the North Island, Mt Ruapehu (2796 m) has an explosive history, with eruptions last century spreading ash as far south as Wellington. The simmering crater is strongly acidic and occasionally mud and rock are thrown down the mountainside. Part of a volcanic chain extending as far as Tonga, extensive seismic measuring equipment ensures ample warning is received of any impending explosion.

INTERNET
www.ruapehu.tourism.co.nz
www.chateau.co.nz

Whakapapa Ski Field
Mordor and the Emyn Muil

Pierre Vinet

Orcs gather to attack at the Battle of the Last Alliance.

In winter, Whakapapa Ski Field is a playground for skiers who enjoy the après-ski lifestyle. In other seasons it is transformed into an area of mountainous volcanic rock.

To visit the area used to portray the battle marking the end of the Second Age of Middle-earth, drive to Iwikau Village, fifteen minutes up the slope from the Grand Chateau. The location is easily accessible but stout walking shoes are recommended. With blasted volcanic rock, steep bluffs and ash, little imagination is required to envisage *Mordor*.

From the main building head north around the learners' ski slope towards Pinnacle Ridge. Before climbing this, walk slightly downhill and along the ridge to a viewpoint of a tumbled area with steep escarpments. As it's hard to be specific about this location, the GPS coordinates are the only precise direction. The slopes and nearby car park saw Orcs attacking Elves and Men, with *Elrond* standing fast. The special-effects team at Weta Studios then added thousands of other 'actors' to complete the scene.

The Great Battle of the Last Alliance was an effort by Elves and Men to rid the world of Sauron's great evil. The second largest army to muster in Middle-earth met a huge Orc host upon Dagorlad Plain in 3431 (SA). Sauron retreated to Barad-dûr and for seven years the alliance laid siege. In the year 3441(SA) he emerged to do battle and in the conflict the Elven king Gil-galad was destroyed but Isildur managed to cut the ring from Sauron's finger before perishing.

Special care was undertaken during filming in all sensitive ecological areas and many acres of carpet were laid out for the Orcs and Elves to walk on, protecting the ground underneath.

The rocky outcrop known as Meads Wall beside Pinnacle Ridge was used in the emotionally charged scene in *The Two Towers* where *Frodo* and *Sam* capture *Gollum*. Actor Andy Serkis (in special clothing) was filmed climbing down the

Ian Brodie

Ian Brodie

Above: The rocky path Gollum leads Frodo and Sam down in the Emyn Muil can be reached from behind the Aorangi Ski Club.

Left: A brooding Mt Ngaruahoe as seen from the Chateau.

Ian Brodie

On a gloomy day this rocky outcrop near Meads Wall becomes a scene straight from the pages of *The Lord of the Rings*.

rocky face and jumping onto the Hobbits. The scene was then mixed at Weta Studios to create *Gollum* from the actor's actual movements.

This area was also used to show the Hobbits lost in the rocky wasteland of the *Emyn Muil* as they tried to find a way down to the blasted plain of *Dagorlad* and on to the *Black Gates*.

Scrambling around the rocks in this area, it is very easy to immerse onself in *Mordor*, the desolate and tortured land from which *Sauron* planned to wage his final war to win domination over Middle-earth. It is particularly eerie to visit when the weather is overcast and clouds swirl around the peaks. Within this basin a number of close-up scenes were also shot portraying the Hobbits' epic trek through *Mordor* towards *Mount Doom*.

Although filming was not undertaken in winter, the high altitude and unpredictable weather were major aspects in all scenes shot in this area.

Mordor (Sindarin 'Black-land') was an inhospitable and barren part of Middle-earth, naturally enclosed on three sides by precipitous mountain ranges. Within this land lay the volcano Orodruin (Sindarin 'Burning Mountain') where The One Ring was forged by Sauron during the Second Age. Mordor was occupied by Sauron for many thousands of years from early in the Second Age until it became abandoned after the Battle of the Last Alliance. Deserted for almost three thousand years, Sauron returned in 2951(TA) and reconstructed his evil fortress of Barad-dûr (Sindarin 'Dark Tower').

VIEWPOINT OF ROCK WHERE ISILDUR CUT THE RING FROM SAURON: S39° 14.116'—E175° 33.529'
ROCK WALL LOCATION OF ABOVE: S39° 14.114'—E175° 33.522'

Ohakune *Ithilien and Mordor*

New Line Productions

Gollum catching his fish in the cold waters behind Mangawhero Falls.

To reach the next location, take a short drive to the village of Ohakune, where the rich volcanic soil lays claim to the largest production area of carrots in New Zealand. Unless skiing is on your agenda, winter isn't the best time to visit. During the colder months the town bustles as the many bars and restaurants swell with skiers reliving the day's runs and spills on the slopes. The 'O' Bar staff remember the filming in this locality very well; the establishment was the scene of a serious party, held to celebrate its completion.

The cast and crew used Ohakune as base for a number of weeks of filming. Many stayed at the Powderhorn Chateau and enjoyed their time in the two restaurants and the very popular Powderhorn Bar. The hotel is the perfect base to visit *Ithilien* and *Mordor* with the added advantage that you might even stay in the same room as Orlando Bloom, Elijah Wood or Peter Jackson.

The Mangawhero River ambles past right outside and from the hotel there are some very pleasant walks you can undertake along its banks. The Maori name Mangawhero literally means 'red stream' and is named for the red algae that grows on the volcanic rocks in the area.

Ian Brodie

Above: The barren
wastes of Mordor.

Opposite: Gollum's
pool, near
Mangawhero Falls.

To reach *Ithilien* travel up the Turoa Ski Field road (also known as the Ohakune Mountain Road Scenic Drive). After much fundraising and work by volunteers, the Ohakune Mountain Road opened in 1963. There are a number of walks and tramps off this road (again visit the local DOC Centre for more information). The road climbs steadily, providing great views of Mt Ruapehu in one direction and the rolling hills around Ohakune in the other.

The exact filming site is accessible after travelling up the road through the beautiful mountain beech as far as the Mangawhero Falls. After parking in the turn-off area clamber down to the riverbed. It was here that *Sméagol* chased and caught a fish, much to his delight. Looking towards the waterfall itself the rocky stream bed scene is readily apparent but for the final film cut the background hills were replaced by a matte painting of much larger peaks.

The hidden outpost of Henneth Annûn (Sindarin 'Window of the Sunset') was constructed by Gondor as a strategic base from which to undertake guerrilla operations against the Harad and Orcs of Sauron. Accessed by a secret passage from the forest it consisted of a number of caves hidden by a high waterfall and was used in later years by the Rangers of Ithilien as both a refuge and base.

44

The day this scene was shot coincided with an unseasonable snowfall. After the local fire brigade washed the snow away Andy Serkis had to don a heavy wetsuit and swim across the pool. Andy recalls Peter Jackson saying 'That was great but let's do it again,' and wondering if he was going to have a heart attack in the freezing conditions.

The scene showing *Sam* and *Frodo* walking through an open glade with a ruined column was filmed just upstream. It can be reached by crossing the stream and walking 50 m into a small clearing, with trees surrounding an open area of springy grass.

In Ohakune you can take a helicopter tour with Wanganui Aerowork, visiting some of the sites used to portray *Mordor*. As most of these cannot be reached by road a helicopter is the only means of access. Departing from outside the Powderhorn Chateau your flight will take you around Mt Ruapehu to where Sam discarded his pots and pans on the climb up *Mt Doom* and provide general views of this amazing volcanic area. You will also visit Whakapapa and fly over the steaming crater lake of Mt Ruapehu. The flight is one of contrasts — from primeval forests to lava blasted rock to azure blue lakes.

Returning to Ohakune, the *River Anduin* is an hour's drive away via Waiouru and then south on SH1 to Taihape, where the National Army Museum at Waiouru makes a worthwhile visit.

To our most gracious hosts . . . The Powderhorn stands alone in my mind as the single most nurturing oasis on this Sacred Island. Nestled in the crisp mountain air, beckoning us forever to return. You rival our most memorable elf retreats.

SEAN ASTIN
POWDERHORN CHATEAU
VISITORS' BOOK

Ian Brodie

Pierre Vinet

Rangitikei River Gorge *River Anduin*

Rangitikei River Rafting

A Rangitikei River Raft floats gently down the Anduin.

The *River Anduin* in the *Fellowship of the Ring* incorporated four different New Zealand rivers, the Rangitikei River near Taihape appearing first. A young river in geological terms, the Rangitikei has carved sheer cliff walls on its way to the Tasman Sea.

The quickest way to approach the location is to drive a little way south from Taihape and turn left at Ohotu. A bungy jump (the highest in the North Island) is situated near the location so follow the 'Hightime Bungy' signs for approximately 15 minutes on a charming scenic drive through bush with scenes of 'heartland' New Zealand. After reaching the bungy site park your car and walk across the one-way traffic bridge. An amazing scene is revealed, as the unspoiled river appears 80 m below, flowing through a gorge of enormous proportions.

The Moawhango River, at its confluence with the Rangitikei, was also used to portray the *Anduin* and as you return to the main road cross via the next one-way bridge. Park at the far end and walk back onto it for another scene of a steep fern-lined gorge with the Moawhango rushing towards the Rangitikei.

INTERNET
www.riveradventures.net.nz

Ian Brodie

View from the
bridge at Hightime
Bungy.

To make your own trip down the *Anduin* drive south 18 km to Mangaweka. Beneath the distinctive DC-3 café is the headquarters of Rangitikei River Rafting. River safety specialists for the filming in this area, they offer a full day eco-tour entitled 'Grand Canyons of the Rangitikei' past the exact site. Suitable for all ages, their oar-powered rafts mean you can sit back and enjoy the scenery as you drift quietly downstream. Your tour will also reveal the wonders of concretionary boulders and ancient shellfish of a past era.

BRIDGE OVER RIVER ANDUIN
S39° 42.279'—E175° 58.238'

Waitarere Forest
Trollshaw Forest and Osgiliath Wood

Pierre Vinet

Situated west of Rivendell, the Trollshaw Forest was the haunt of Trolls who travelled down from the Ettenmoors. In the year 2941 (TA) Bilbo Baggins was captured by three trolls but managed to keep them arguing until the sun rose and they turned to stone.

Above: Frodo and Sam in the forests of Ithilien.

Right: Waitarere Forest tracks are suitable for mountain bikes.

INTERNET
www.rivernz.com

Waitarere Forest is located south of Foxton on the Kapiti Coast. From the north, after passing Poroutawhao watch for the turning to Waitarere Beach on your right. The Kapiti Coast is a popular summer holiday area for many Wellingtonians who come to relax at the many beaches along the coast. Waitarere Beach is a typical beach village with the ever-present camping grounds and ice-cream parlours.

Just as you enter Waitarere a small unnamed side road on the right allows entry to a parking area on the edge of the forest. Vehicle access is not permitted any further, which provides good justification for a walk on any of a number of well-formed tracks under the tall trees.

The plantation forest stretches for some kilometres both north and south of Waitarere and is very different to native bush, with most of the trails also suitable for mountain bikes. Filming took place in different parts of the park, including *Osgiliath Wood* where *Frodo*, *Sam* and *Sméagol* walked after leaving *Faramir*, *Trollshaw Forest*, *Arwen* walking through the trees and Gandalf and Pippin riding to *Minas Tirith*.

Ian Brodie

Otaki and Otaki Gorge
leaving the Shire

The town of Otaki, a one-hour drive north of Wellington, is rich in both sunshine and history. Maori settlement of the area was as early as the 1300s and the small village continued its peaceful existence until 1819, when the Ngati Toa invasion (under the famous chief Te Rauparaha) culminated in the Battle of Waiorua in 1826. With Te Rauparaha established as paramount chief there was constant inter-tribal fighting but in 1839 the missionary Octavius Hadfield arrived from the Bay of Islands, in an attempt to restore peace through 'Christianisation'.

Gandalf the Grey leading the Hobbits away from the Shire.

By 1886 the railway had reached the expanding village bringing an influx of settlers to mill timber, clear land and continue to extend the railway. Farming developed in the ensuing years and in the late 1930s a number of market gardeners moved north to produce the ever-increasing quantities of fruit and vegetables required for the city markets.

Today Otaki is almost a dormitory city of Wellington, with commuters making the hour-long trip to Wellington each day, although market gardening and farming are still major industries.

The nearby Otaki Gorge Road was used to portray the young Hobbits' journey to the border of their beloved *Shire* through peaceful and productive gardens and farms, providing an interesting parallel with Otaki's real-life industries.

The turn-off to the Otaki Gorge is on the left just south of Otaki after crossing the Otaki River. Initially sealed, it soon becomes a narrow unpaved road so care should be taken over the 19-km journey, especially for drivers who are not used to driving in these conditions.

Although the specific locations used to show the Hobbits leaving the *Shire* in *The Fellowship of the Ring* are not accessible to the public, the trip to the Otaki Gorge is

49

Pierre Vinet

highly recommended. The transformation of scenery during the short drive up the gorge is quite remarkable, and provides a useful insight into exactly why New Zealand proved to be the perfect place to film *The Lord of the Rings* trilogy. Leaving the rolling farm country behind, the road soon narrows and plunges into beautiful rimu and rata bush. Breaks in the bush on the side of the road reveal glimpses of the Otaki River as it flows through the gorge on its way to the Tasman Sea.

The scenery here is very reminiscent of Tolkien's description of the outer reaches of the *Shire* and once the end of the road is reached there are a number of excellent picnic spots beside the river, with the bush providing cool and welcome relief from the hot summer sun.

New Zealand is the ideal place to shoot these films. The land mass is so young, so savage, so untamed and unruly, all of which make it special.

CATE BLANCHETT

In another interesting parallel, a four-day tramp is also available from this end of the road, climbing across the Tararua Range to the Kaitoke Regional Park in Upper Hutt, parts of which were used to portray *Rivendell*.

51

Paraparaumu *the Pelennor Fields*

The ability to film different locations for the same scene and then combine them together seamlessly is part of the film-makers' wizardry and the epic *Battle of the Pelennor Fields* is a perfect example of their artistry. Although all wide shots for the battle were filmed in the middle of the South Island near Twizel (see page 100) many of the close-ups were filmed at Queen Elizabeth Park near Paraparaumu, only 45 minutes north of Wellington.

> The Pelennor (Sindarin 'Enclosed-lands') was the name given to the fertile lands surrounding the Gondorian city of Minas Tirith. Enclosed by the defensive wall called the Rammas Echor (Sindarin 'Encircling Walls'), it was here that the largest conflagration during the Third Age of Middle-earth took place — the Battle of the Pelennor Fields.

If you are heading south to Wellington from Otaki you can drive into the park at MacKays Crossing, which is just south of Paraparaumu. As much of the filming was undertaken with a blue-screen background there is nothing very recognisable but it was in these paddocks that both the downed *Nazgûl* and *mûmakil* were filmed. A walk in the park or along the nearby beach makes a pleasant diversion and it is worth pausing at the American Memorial, which commemorates the large number of US Marines based here during World War II.

The name Paraparaumu is Maori and possibly refers to the arrival of a war party who found only a few scraps of food in abandoned earth ovens, as parapara means food scraps, and an umu is an earth oven.

A dead Mûmak after the Battle of the Pelennor Fields.

Pierre Vinet

Wellington

Totally Wellington

To any enthusiast of *The Lord of the Rings* films, Wellington is Production Central, home to Peter Jackson, 3 Foot 6, Wingnut Films, Weta Workshop and Weta Digital. As Peter Jackson has said: 'I feel incredibly proud that this country, and especially this town, is responsible for what we have done.'

Bookshops promote Tolkien in their front window, Orcs produced by Sideshow Weta stare back from specialty-shop windows and there's even a Minister of Middle-earth.

Wellington nestles between a magnificent harbour and forest-clad hills, creating a compact downtown area with an intimacy uncommon in many other cities.

The earliest name for Wellington is Te Upoko o te ika a Maui, which means the head of Maui's fish. The Polynesian explorer, Kupe, is credited with the initial

Wellington Harbour with the botanical gardens in the foreground. Reference photos of trees from here were used to create the ents. Treebeard is modelled on a pohutukawa.

INTERNET
www.wellingtonNZ.com

53

Downtown Wellington.

Totally Wellington

discovery of Wellington Harbour around the tenth century. The first European settlement was named Wellington after the first Duke of Wellington, by the directors of the New Zealand Company, whose first vessel arrived in 1839.

In November 1863 a resolution was moved by Parliament, then situated in Auckland, that a more central site was needed for the capital and the first sitting was held in Wellington on 26 July 1865.

Fire and earthquakes have since destroyed many early buildings but for those with an interest in early architecture the Nairn Street Cottage (68 Nairn Street) is a survivor from 1858. Also worthy of a visit is the Government Building on Lambton Quay; designed to look like stone, it is constructed entirely of wood. Nearby Parliament House and the Beehive should be included in any itinerary with daily tours available.

Wellington — downtown sites

The centre of downtown Wellington is very easy to negotiate so put on some walking shoes and spend a day visiting some famous and interesting sights. A good place to start is the Museum of New Zealand, Te Papa Tongarewa, on Cable Street. Receiving worldwide acclaim for its exciting modern approach, the museum features a number of 'hands-on' exhibitions. Admission is free but charges apply to some exhibitions.

On the corner of Jervois Quay and Cable Street is The Film Centre, New Zealand's Museum of the Moving Image, and well worth a look. Admission is free. Nearby at 10 Kent Terrace is the Embassy, Wellington's grandest cinema, venue for the Australasian premieres of both *The Fellowship of the Ring* and *The Two Towers*, and the World Premiere of *The Return of the King* in 2003. The Embassy has recently been refurbished and features many refinements, which have seen the grand old theatre restored to its former glory. Boasting New Zealand's largest screen and superb digital sound, watching a movie here is an experience not to be missed.

For those wishing a more permanent souvenir of 'Wellywood' walk around to Dymocks Booksellers at 360 Lambton Quay. They have the largest range of Tolkien books in New Zealand and stock the Sideshow Weta collectible figures.

Te Papa Tongarewa.

Totally Wellington

In December 2001 the red carpet was rolled out and Ringwraiths rode on horseback when the Embassy Cinema hosted the Australasian premiere of The Fellowship of the Ring. To quote Elijah Wood, 'They said it was going to be massive and suddenly I felt like a rock star . . .'

A more unusual location is the WestpacTrust Stadium on the waterfront. During the lunch break in a one-day cricket match between New Zealand and England, Peter Jackson extolled the crowd of 30,000 to stamp and chant in the Black Speech. The sounds were used for the Orcs' chants during the Battle of Helm's Deep.

Mt Victoria
escape from the Nazgûl

Pierre Vinet

The green tunnel leads to a frightening encounter for the Hobbits.

While on paper the centre of a metropolitan area may seem to be an unlikely location for the rural *Shire*, Mt Victoria's role in *The Fellowship of the Ring* movie is a direct result of the foresight of Wellington's town planners. With a superb view from the summit — stretching from Cook Strait in the south to the city of Wellington in the north — Mt Victoria is part of an encircling green belt. Its forests and landscape provided the perfect location for the *Outer Shire*, along with easy accessibility for the cast and crew, something that wasn't always easy to achieve. It also marked the commencement of shooting on 11 October 1999, and the beginning of a 274-day journey that would take the cast and crew throughout the country.

The easiest way to reach the locations is to drive along Alexandra Road, which eventually takes you to the summit. The road has several parking areas, so watch for one on your left 1.2 km from the intersection onto Alexandra Road, on a sweeping right-hand turn. The track on the left-hand side of the road, and to your right, plunges downhill through a forest and after another right-hand turn the view ahead is instantly recognisable.

Like a green tunnel the straight path leads through two banks with dark overhanging trees, and no imagination is required to picture *Frodo* standing in the middle of the path, listening fearfully for the approaching *Nazgûl*. The city below is invisible, the area one of quiet solitude with rustling trees and chirping insects completing this scene of a rural path in the *Shire*.

Continue down the same path and as it turns to the right two further locations unfold. The steep bank on your left marks the spot where the Hobbits slid down to discover a feast of mushrooms.

LOCATION OF PATH
S 41° 18.101'—E 174° 47.293'

56

Ian Brodie

Pierre Vinet

Above: The ridge on Mt Victoria used to film the race to the ferry.

Left: The Hobbits take refuge from the Nazgûl as they flee the Shire.

Ian Brodie

The location for a
perfect Hobbit-
hiding place.

On your right up the hill are two trees with a small overhanging ledge. Here a large manufactured tree was transplanted to provide a more realistic root system for the Hobbits to hide under. It was here the frightened Hobbits hid to escape the *Nazgûl*, with the worms and spiders escaping from the ground in revulsion at his evilness.

There are parts that are really like Scotland — only bigger! Maybe it's Scotland as seen by a Hobbit!

BILLY BOYD

The path winds down through the woods towards the city and on a warm summer's day, the scent of pine needles and the tall trees standing against a blue sky create an idyllic and surprisingly peaceful spot.

Unit Publicist Claire Raskind-Cooper recalls how the press had discovered this area was to be used for the first day of filming. 'I remember running up the bank asking the photographers to move back.'

LOCATION OF TREE HOBBITS
HID UNDER:
S 41° 18.075'—E 174° 47.319'

(NB these coordinates are
from the path)

Pierre Vinet

Mt Victoria and Lyall Bay *Dunharrow*

A visit to the *Rohirrim* encampment of *Dunharrow* can also be achieved whilst visiting Mt Victoria. Although wide shots were filmed in the South Island, close-ups were filmed at 'Mt Vic' and nearby Lyall Bay. To visit the Mt Victoria location travel down Cambridge Terrace (past the Embassy) to the Basin Reserve. As you reach here turn immediately left (before going through the road tunnel) and drive to the top of the very steep Ellice Street. Parking is very limited and it is possible to walk down through the park from Alexandra Road.

Dunharrow (Dark-burial-place) was one of the few remnants of an ancient race of men still left in Middle-earth. A burial tomb and complex, it was constructed well before the rise of Gondor and the return of the Númenoreans. Set high on the mountain known as the Dwimorberg, this large field served as the assembly area for the Rohirrim but also marked the entrance to the Dimholt and the dreaded Paths of the Dead.

This disused quarry was remodelled into *Dunharrow* with the addition of a number of *Rohirrim* tents and a path laid through the middle. It was here that *Dernhelm* approached *Merry* prior to their epic ride to the aid of the *Gondorians*.

Additional scenes were shot at Lyall Bay, which is immediately beside the airport facing Cook Strait. Drive around Lyall Bay on the Island Bay Road and park beside the sea at Dorrie Leslie Park. The cliff face in the fenced off area was utilised as *Dunharrow*. Further along at Red Rocks is where Frodo, Sam and Gollum cowered at the Black Gate.

Ian Brodie

Cliff faces and trees at the top of Ellice Street provided the perfect location for Dunharrow.

The Wairarapa — an introduction

The Wairarapa covers a wide area with a diverse range of spectacular landscapes. Situated an hour north of Wellington, it's a popular escape with vineyards, adventure activities and tourist trails. The vineyards also became a popular haunt for the *Lord of the Rings* cast.

Driving north on SH2 the urban areas of the Hutt Valley are soon replaced by bush-covered hills as the road climbs over the Rimutaka Ranges. A spectacular route, the road ascends through a number of valleys before reaching the summit, with fabulous views of Featherston and the Wairarapa.

View from the summit of the Rimutaka Ranges road.

The Rimutaka Ranges proved a major obstacle until the railway arrived in Featherston in 1878. This was no ordinary train track, and the steepness of the climb required a friction-drive system. Designed by John Fell, the Fell Engine featured

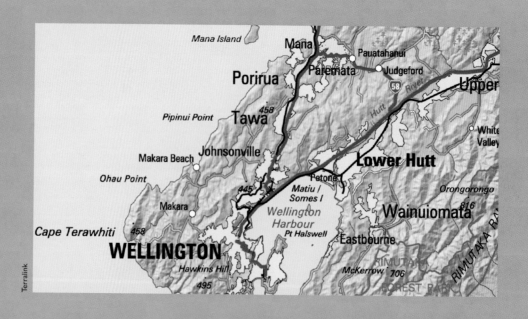

smooth horizontal powered wheels held against a raised centre-rail that pulled the train up the Incline. Operating from 1878 to 1955, the high cost of operations necessitated the construction of a tunnel through the ranges. The 8.798 km tunnel opened on 29 October 1955 and the dutiful little Fell Engines were cut up for scrap. Only one survived, now on display in the Fell Museum at Featherston, and beautifully restored to her former glory.

Ian Brodie

Featherston has grown considerably since the opening of the Rimutaka Tunnel and residents now travel to work in the Hutt Valley and Wellington.

Featherston is also host to Fernside, one of New Zealand's finest historic homes. To stay in this magnificent residence is a tonic in itself, but the other reason for a stay here is to wander the gardens of *Lothlórien*.

Lothlórien, realm of Celeborn and Galadriel.

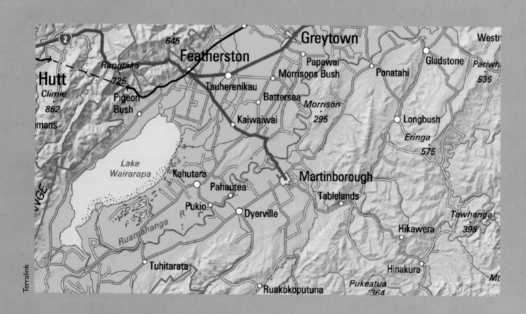

Terralink

Fernside *Lothlórien and the Gladden Fields*

Pierre Vinet

Fernside provides an opportunity to drift back to the peace and tranquillity of a bygone era. Created by Ella and Charles Elgar in 1924 to satisfy Mrs Elgar's wish to entertain the rich and influential, Fernside is a gracious home with large rooms including a library, dining and drawing rooms. Accommodation is available in one of four original en-suite bedrooms and rooms are also available for private functions.

The gardens are an absolute delight and it's no wonder they were chosen to portray *Lothlórien*. In the style of English garden designer Gertrude Jekyll, they feature a number of 'garden rooms' with their own distinctive plantings. The man-made lake was used to portray the departure from *Lothlórien* as well as scenes depicting *Sméagol* and *Déagol* fishing near the *Gladden Fields*, which appeared in *The Return of the King*.

Although not filmed, the wooded walks are beautiful, especially in the autumn. To walk under the golden trees with fallen leaves underfoot is an absolute delight.

Note: this site is not open to the public. These locations are only accessible by staying in the house. Refer to the website for further information.

Lothlórien (Sindarin 'Dream-flower') had been the dwelling of the high Elven queen Galadriel, the Lady of Lórien, for thousands of years. Situated beside the River Celebrant west of the Anduin, the realm of Galadriel and Celeborn was home to the gold and silver mellyrn trees. The Elves dwelt in the boughs upon platforms (talan) and were also called the Galadhrim, or tree people.

Above: Sméagol and Déagol fishing near the Gladden Fields.

Right: The Celebrant flows through Lothlórien.

INTERNET
www.fernside.co.nz

Pierre Vinet

Above: An elven boat and seat beside the Celebrant at Fernside.

Left: The bridge as it appears at Fernside, without its Elven arches.

The Putangirua Pinnacles
the Dimholt Road

The tortuous landscape of the Putangirua riverbed.

One of the most unusual geographical landscapes in New Zealand accessible by car is the Putangirua Pinnacles on the south coast of the Wairarapa. To really enjoy a visit to this area it's best to stay overnight in the small town of Martinborough. Surrounded by vineyards and olive trees, the Victorian buildings here are home to some great restaurants where you can sample the local cuisine. There is also the opportunity to spend a night in the historic Martinborough Hotel, where Cate Blanchett and other cast stayed whilst filming at nearby Fernside.

The drive to Putangirua takes about 45 minutes heading south on Pirinoa Road and then turning left towards Cape Palliser. After reaching the rugged coast it is a short drive to the Department of Conservation (DOC) car park. There is also a camping ground here for those with a tent and time to enjoy the opportunity to relive an aspect of *Aragorn*'s epic journey.

Named The Paths of the Dead by the Rohirrim, this road was constructed by the builders of Dunharrow, early in the Second Age. Leading from Dunharrow under the Dwimorberg to the south, the haunted way was closed to all but the Army of the Dead and the heir of Isildur.

There are three different walks to the pinnacles. One of the most spectacular (and the best way to reach the filming locations) is the walk up the Putangirua streambed. Although the hike isn't hard the return trip can take 2–3 hours, so some provisions should be carried.

The 'badlands erosion' that is the special feature here was formed over time as the streambed exposed layers of gravel to rain and floods. Some rocks remain more resistant and form pinnacles or 'hoodoos'.

It is within the shadows of these eerie columns that *Legolas* tells the chilling story of the *Army of the Dead* in *The Return of the King*.

Upper Hutt — an introduction

The diversity of landscape in the Upper Hutt region made it ideal for filming for a number of reasons.

The proximity of nearby studios minimised Peter Jackson's logistical problems of flying hundreds of people to other parts of the country, often for only a short scene.

The town of Upper Hutt is a pleasant 40-minute drive through the Hutt Valley from Wellington and makes an ideal base from which to explore the region. Away from cosmopolitan Wellington, Upper Hutt has a smaller village feel, with all the facilities one would expect to find in a major city.

The Hutt Valley has been continuously occupied for over 800 years and when the people of Te Ati Awa arrived they used the river as both a source of plentiful food and an efficient transport route, naming it Te Awa Kairangi, or 'highly esteemed river'.

European settlers arrived in the region in 1839 but the Valley grew slowly, mainly due to the swampy nature of the land. This all changed dramatically when a major earthquake in 1855 raised the level of the Hutt Valley and drained the surrounding wetland, making it suitable for farming.

Above top: The Hutt River.

Above: Kaitoke Regional Park.

Today, the city of Upper Hutt occupies a large area and its numerous parks, native bush reserves and river combine with easy access to make it a very pleasant suburban city. There are a number of indoor and outdoor attractions in the area as well as a superb boutique cinema called The Lighthouse. It's almost like watching movies at home; seating fewer than 40 people it features a large screen and excellent sound.

INTERNET
www.uhcc.govt.nz

Kaitoke Regional Park
Rivendell and the Fords of Isen

Ian Brodie

Kaitoke Regional Park nestles in the foothills of the Tararua Ranges, 12 km north of Upper Hutt. The park contains some 2800 hectares of mature native forest and is popular for picnics, swimming and walking, with more than 100,000 visitors enjoying the area each year.

To enter the park turn off SH2 and travel down Waterworks Road to the Pakuratahi – Hutt Forks car park. There are four different walks beginning near here to choose from, in addition to many pleasant picnic spots along the rivers and bush fringes. Camping is available on the grassy flats at Kaitoke where toilets and coin-operated barbecues are also available. The beautiful clear pools on the Hutt and Pakuratahi Rivers are ideal for swimming during the summer months.

Rivendell was a translation of the Sindarin name Imladris (deep cloven valley) and was situated in the foothills of the western Misty Mountains. Elrond founded this refuge in the wilderness (the Last Homely House East of the Sea) in 1797 (SA) after retreating from the evil of Sauron.

The position of *Rivendell* is signposted from the entrance to the park and at the location itself there is an interpretative display showing the construction and final result. Although most exterior shots were digitally rendered, the set constructors built a large set here, including the bedroom where *Frodo* recovered from his knife attack. The impressive site included purpose-built scaffolding which continued out into the river, along with a man-made river and waterfalls to suit the film-makers' exacting requirements.

Above: Area set aside for dressing rooms, Kaitoke Regional Park.

Over 30 workers began construction in November 1999, completing the set in March 2000, in time for filming which took place between April and May 2000. During filming there were more than 300 crew on site. The river, as seen from the nearby bridge, portrayed *The Fords of Isen* in the extended DVD of *The Two Towers*.

Opposite: Luxuriant foliage — Rivendell.

Ian Brodie

INTERNET	RIVENDELL SITE: S 41° 03.438'—E 175° 11.666'
www.wrc.govt.nz	DRESSING ROOMS ETC: S 41° 03.446'—E 174° 11.617'

Harcourt Park *Isengard Gardens*

Pierre Vinet

Above: Gandalf the Grey and Saruman the White in the gardens of Isengard.

Right: Gandalf the Grey arrives at Isengard.

To travel from *Rivendell* to *Isengard* was an arduous journey of many weeks with countless leagues of wild rough country to negotiate but in Upper Hutt it can be completed in less than 15 minutes. A pleasant oasis in suburbia, Harcourt Park was utilised for three different *Isengard* scenes and is situated on Akatarawa Road; a right turn off SH2 if returning from Kaitoke. There is accommodation available right next door at the Harcourt Holiday Park.

An elevated section of the park was transformed into the gardens of *Isengard* where *Gandalf* and *Saruman* first met after the rediscovery of the ring at *Hobbiton*. It is located across a green lawn and up a small rise with a park-bench situated at the top. Looking down from the garden you can see another two sites, although virtually nothing now remains to mark the spot. At the time of writing a slightly discernable track (mainly noticeable by the change in grass colour) could be seen running through the middle of the lawn. During filming, the lawn was removed and a gravel pathway formed complete with a chain-link fence on each side. Sound familiar? It was the entrance road into *Isengard*. Once the scenes were completed it was totally removed and the lawn replanted, a tribute to the care and attention of *The Lord of the Rings* crew.

ISENGARD GARDENS
S 41° 06.069'—E 175° 05.644'

Pierre Vinet

Harcourt Park *the Orc Tree*

Chris Coad

Harcourt Park is also home to the famous hinged trees of *Isengard*. During the transformation of *Saruman*'s lair a number of trees needed to be filmed being cut down to provide fuel for his furnaces.

These scenes would need to be filmed a number of times and the set designers took a novel approach. First of all, two trees were cut down from a remote location and transported (roots and all) over 200 km, with each section of cut branch numbered to enable re-assembly.

Two holes were dug and iron poles driven into the ground, and the trees reassembled by bolting all the branches together before they were 'planted' attached to the iron poles and effectively hinged. This meant they could be 'cut' down, brought back up and 'cut' down again while being filmed from a different angle. As the trees didn't have enough leaves, a team spent two weeks wiring on plastic ones.

Ian Brodie

Above top: Saruman's Orcs wasted no time in felling the beautiful trees of Isengard.

Above: The same scene today is certainly less terrifying.

The results were spectacular. Filmed in the rain, the trees toppled on command (after a few teething troubles) and after a week of filming some spectacular footage was obtained and mixed digitally to portray the infamous makeover of *Isengard*. The trees have since been removed.

Unrelated to *The Lord of the Rings*, this park is also home to one of the best examples of an earthquake fault line in New Zealand. The Wellington Fault passes through the park and in the nineteenth century a large earthquake shook this area, lifting the ground some 5 m and diverting the course of the Hutt River. The fault, which is signposted within the park and visited regularly by geology students, is well worth a visit.

| SMALLER HINGED TREE: S 41° 06.109'—E 175° 05.612' |
| LARGER HINGED TREE: S 41° 06.109'—E 175° 05.624' |

Ian Brodie

Above: The garden at Harcourt Park where Gandalf and Saruman walked.

Right: This shot of Orthanc comprises three locations — mountains from Glenorchy, a park in Upper Hutt and a digital model.

New Line Productions

Hutt River *River Anduin and Rohan River*

The Hutt River flows for some 30 km from its source in the Southern Tararua Ranges through bush, farmland and city before finally entering the sea at Petone. Activity along the Wellington Fault over the last 2 million years helped form the river, shattering and weakening the underlying bedrock and forming the associated floodplain. The river was an important transport link for both Maori and European settlers and a foot track followed its banks for many kilometres before continuing over the Rimutaka Hill to the Wairarapa. Remnants of the original vegetation remain on its banks in many places and its natural beauty provided an ideal site for filming the *River Anduin*, close to the Wellington studios.

Principal filming was undertaken on the river between Moonshine and Totara Park although further smaller scenes were shot at Kaitoke in the north. The river can be accessed off SH2. After crossing the Moonshine Bridge (heading north) watch for the access road on your left just past Poet's Park. The small Elven boats were launched into the river here many times, with a number of close shots of the travellers originating from this locality.

Another great way to follow the river is to walk all or part of the Hutt River Trail starting at Petone in the south and ending 24 km later in Upper Hutt. An access point at the Moonshine Bridge enables a short stroll along the bank to Totara Park.

The scene where *Aragorn* was washed ashore after his encounter with the *Wargs* in *Rohan* was filmed on another portion of the Hutt River. To reach it, turn left off the main highway (SH2) approximately 2 km north of Upper Hutt on to Topaz Street. At the next roundabout turn right into Gemstone Drive and a little way down on the right there is public access via a small driveway to the river.

Above top: The Fellowship travel down the Anduin to Amon Hen.

Above: The Hutt River, far from where the rest of the scene was shot, near Queenstown.

HUTT RIVER VIEWING AREA:
S 41° 07.115'—E175° 02.543'

Pierre Vinet

Ian Brodie

Wellington — a day tour

Above: A detail of Elvish architecture at Rivendell.

Below: Saruman the White, before his downfall into evil.

A day tour of the locations in and around Wellington is easily achieved and will allow you to see a diverse range of geography as well as some of the most easily recognisable scenes. Grab a map, make an early start and drive initially to Kent Terrace for a look at the Embassy Theatre — location of the Australasian Premieres of *The Fellowship of the Ring* and *The Two Towers*. Continue on to Pirie Street, park your car just prior to entering the bus tunnel, and venture into the wooded Mt Victoria town belt for a wander around the outskirts of the *Shire* and the *Race to the Ferry*.

To maintain your sustenance and savour the tastiest brunch in town, head to the Chocolate Fish Café. Once you're suitably replenished return to Wellington City and drive out on the motorway (SH2) to Kaitoke Regional Park and the location of *Rivendell*.

Down the road is Harcourt Park in Upper Hutt, which became the *Gardens of Isengard* in 2000. Trees, gardens and picnic spots abound as well as the location of the famous 'hinged' trees of *Isengard*.

The nearby Hutt River from Moonshine Bridge to Poet's Park was used for close-filming of the Fellowship on the *River Anduin* and is ideal for a short stroll before returning to Wellington. Pause at Dry Creek Quarry at the bottom of Haywards Hill to see the set for *Helm's Deep* and *Minas Tirith*.

Dinner at Leuven on Featherston Street should replenish even the most famished before returning to the Embassy Theatre to catch one of your favourite films, the ideal end to a day of adventure and discovery. Wellington hosts an excellent public transportation system and all of these locations are accessible by bus or train, although you would need to allow more time than if travelling by car.

Wellington — cafés and entertainment

Based in Wellington for an extended period, the cast found plenty of opportunities to let off steam.

It's easy to see why one of the most popular locations for the crew was the Chocolate Fish Café, situated at Scorching Bay. Close to Seatoun where the cast lived during filming, it provides excellent food and good service with a little eccentricity — the Chocolate Fish must be one of the few restaurants in the world with a main street running through its centre. Occupying a small house, tables are available both inside and out but the best seating is on the other side of the road, right beside the sea. Wearing bright day-glo vests, staff cross the road to deliver food and coffee to their guests 'on the other side'.

If you feel the need for an ice-cream, why not visit the dairy that appears in the short film *The Long and Short Of It* directed by Sean Astin. Appearing in the extended DVD of *The Two Towers*, the dairy is opposite the Rita Angus Retirement Village on Coutts Road in the suburb of Kilbirnie.

Above: At night, Wellington comes alive.

Favourite nightspots of Liv Tyler and Elijah Wood were Brava and Studio 9. Sean Bean frequented Molly Malone's while Viggo Mortensen was content with steak and chips at the Green Parrot.

Below: Prime seating at the Chocolate Fish Café.

New Zealand fashion also played its part; Liv Tyler has been pictured in international fashion magazines wearing Zambesi, a leading New Zealand fashion label. She also shopped in the Wellington fashion design store Starfish.

The Hobbits found another means of relaxation at Lyall Bay, close to Wellington Airport, when first one and then another tried the art of surfing. Within hours all four could be seen riding the waves.

The sets *Bree*

Pierre Vinet

Filmed at Fort Dorset in the suburb of Seatoun, this old army base is not accessible to the public. Nothing remains of the set but those wishing to obtain a view of the base can go to the end of Burnham Street and walk around the beach. This allows a good view without trespassing.

The township of *Bree* was located near the intersection of the *East* and *North Roads* in central *Eriador*. A hamlet of both Hobbits and Men, the *Prancing Pony Inn* was the centre of community life for both the local populace and travellers who frequented the tavern each night to gossip and share stories. A two-day ride from *Hobbiton*, it became the overnight refuge for the four Hobbits as they fled their homeland.

Pierre Vinet

It didn't feel like we were making a big film. It was all happening in Peter Jackson's back yard. His back yard, of course, being New Zealand, which has the most amazing landscapes and people necessary to bring it off.
IAN MCKELLEN

The sets *Helm's Deep*

Ian Brodie

The set has been totally removed but for the curious, travel out on the Western Hutt Road to Haywards Hill Road. The quarry is at the bottom of this hill and is closed to the public.

The fortress of *Helm's Deep* was located in the northern *White Mountains* at the head of the *Deeping Comb*. Although built by *Gondor* it was later occupied by the men of *Rohan* and became a refuge during times of war. *The Tower of the Hornburg, Helm's Gate*, the *Deeping Wall* and *Deeping Tower* were major fortifications guarding the *Aglarond*; a series of caverns reaching back into the hills. Also known as the *Glittering Caves*, these became a place of hiding during the *Battle of Helm's Deep*.

Ah, God bless Wellington! I love it so much.
I want to have a place there that I can go
and visit. It's wonderful. It's home. I mean,
I spent a year and a half of my life there.
ELIJAH WOOD

Pierre Vinet

The sets *Minas Tirith*

Pierre Vinet

Minas Tirith nestled into the quarry slopes of Haywards Hill.

Also constructed at the quarry off Haywards Hill Road was the city of *Minas Tirith*. Nothing now remains and the quarry is fully operational again.

Built at the end of the Second Age, the twin cities of Minas Anor (Sindarin 'Tower of the [Setting] Sun') and Minas Ithil (Sindarin ' Tower of the [Rising] Moon') were two of the founding cities of Gondor. After Minas Ithil was taken by the Nazgûl and renamed Minas Morgul (the Tower of Sorcery) the city that would forever look across Osgiliath towards it was renamed Minas Tirith (Tower of Guard).

Built literally into the side of Mount Mindolluin, Minas Tirith was constructed on seven levels with concentric walls. On a huge abutment (like the prow of a ship) lay the Citadel of Anárion and the Court of the Fountain, 700 feet above the Pelennor Fields.

Above: The amazing
attention to detail is
evident in this close-
up at Minas Tirith.

Left: The body of
Aragorn at Minas
Tirith as seen by
Arwen in her
dream.

Nelson — an introduction

Centre Stage

Centre Stage

Above top: Taste Nelson wines and seafood at Mapua.

Above: The golden sands of Abel Tasman National Park.

INTERNET
www.NelsonNZ.com

With a mild Mediterranean climate, Nelson is well known for its beautiful beaches and bush-clad mountains, and has become the centre for crafts, food and winemaking. Home to three national parks, people visit all year round to tramp, walk, sail and taste.

Nelson was first named Whakatu by Ra Kai Hau Tu, and in later years Pohea established the Matangi Awhio Pa on the edge of the harbour. In the nineteenth century, European settlers created their own piece of Victorian England, still evident today, with many fine old villas standing in streets named Hardy, Brönte, Haven and Wakefield.

The three national parks are easily accessible and offer diverse landscapes. Abel Tasman National Park is New Zealand's only coastal park. Beautiful golden sand beaches are a feature and there are opportunities to experience marine activities including sea kayaking, sailing, cruising and walking the popular Coast Track.

Nelson Lakes National Park is more mountainous and includes the northernmost peaks of the Southern Alps. The park features two gorgeous mountain lakes, with bush and alpine walks, horse treks and fishing trips. In winter visitors ski the Rainbow Valley, which also provides ski touring and alpine climbing.

The second largest national park in New Zealand, Kahurangi National Park, includes the largest remaining area of natural land in the northwestern South Island.

Filming was undertaken in three remote locations and some unique 'props' originated from local craftspeople.

The cast particularly enjoyed their time here, making the most of the idyllic beaches and calm seas.

Nelson — artisans

With over 300 artisans in the region it was no wonder *The Lord of the Rings* prop department looked here for a number of props.

Situated in Richmond, Harrington Brewers were asked to brew a special beer for *Hobbiton* and the *Prancing Pony*. A number were tested before the crew settled on Harrington's Stout. This rich dark stout derives its character from a blend of toasted malts combined with a special strain of yeast. There was one other consideration — the brew had to have an alcohol content of no more than 1.1%. Due to the many takes required to perfect a shot, anything stronger could have had disastrous effects. The result was a good-looking and fine-tasting ale, and over 20,000 litres were provided. The brewery is open to the public and enthusiasts can purchase Harrington's Stout, with an added 5% alcohol by volume.

Each year the Nelson World of Wearable Art Extravaganza showcases unique artworks all centred on one proviso — finished designs must be original, sometimes bizarre, certainly unique, and able to be worn. The World of Wearable Art and Collectable Cars, close to Nelson Airport, features a number of these innovative fashions, many designed by artists who worked on costumes for *The Lord of the Rings*.

Above top: Thorkild Hansen at work.

Above: The One Ring to rule them all.

Jens Hansen Gold and Silversmith is tucked away on Trafalgar Square in central Nelson. Amongst the jeweller's many designs one now eclipses all others. After submitting a design for the *One Ring* to the producers, Jens went on to make 40 rings, one almost 16 cm in diameter, with a similarly scaled gold chain. Sadly, Jens died in 1999 before he could see his masterpiece on screen but his son, Thorkild, continues the family tradition. One of the original rings is on display and Thorkild will craft copies of the *One Ring* in both 9 and 18 ct gold.

INTERNET
www.jenshansen.com

Takaka Hill *Chetwood Forest*

New Line Productions

Ian Brodie

Above top: Frodo and Sam depart the Shire – little realising the adventures that would befall them.

Above: Forest and sinkholes – Takaka Hill.

LOCATION
S40° 57.707'—E172° 53.062'

The two-hour drive to this location is one of unspoilt beaches, striking mountain landscapes and dramatic holes in the earth. After passing through rich orchard areas, stop at Mapua to view the saltwater aquarium. The restaurant across the road serves great coffee and tasty smoked fish — with fresh bread you'll have a lunch to savour in the *Chetwood Forest*.

Pass through Motueka and past the golden sand beach of Kaiteriteri, before climbing to the 972 m summit of Takaka Hill, with its rocky marble outcrops, the only place outside Italy where such formations exist.

Just past the signposted Ngarua Caves watch for the unpaved Canaan Road on your right, which will take you through ghostly trees amidst outcrops of weather-worn marble. Park after crossing the cattle stop 8 km from the main road. Just ahead on your right is where the catering marquee stood and just a little further on past another stand of trees is where *Aragorn* led the Hobbits into the wilds after leaving *Bree*. A further scene showing the Hobbits leaving the *Shire* was also filmed here.

For the energetic, there is a two-hour return walk to Harward's Hole, a 176-m deep, 15-m wide tomo (sinkhole) in the limestone rock, the twelfth largest in the world and the largest in the southern hemisphere. *A note of warning:* keep to the marked paths in this area as a number of other unmarked sinkholes rival the best in *Moria*.

After returning to the main road continue to the summit of Takaka Hill for great views of Golden and Tasman Bays before winding downhill to Takaka, principal point of entry to Abel Tasman National Park. With a number of scenic attractions in the area, you may wish to stay the night.

Fleeing from Bree and the horror of the Black Riders, the Hobbits are led by Aragorn into the Chetwood Forest, northeast of Bree.

Viggo Mortensen

Viggo Mortensen

Above: Chetwood Forest #7 by Viggo Mortensen.

Left: Winter (2000) by Viggo Mortensen.

Mt Olympus *south of Rivendell*

Rocky outcrops on
Mt Olympus.

Ian Brodie

Two of the most spectacular landscapes in *The Fellowship of the Ring* are situated in Kahurangi National Park. The first, on the side of Mt Olympus, would not have appeared at all were it not for the local knowledge of Nelson Helicopters' pilot, Bill Reid. While filming was underway at Takaka, Bill described a place he thought would be ideal to show some of the rough country south of Rivendell. Several months later, when snow made filming at another location impossible, this became where the Fellowship hide from *Saruman*'s *crebain* (black crows from *Dunland*) who were searching for the Nine.

The location is remote and spectacular, and so isolated the only way for the average traveller to reach it is with the help of Nelson Helicopters. This company provided considerable logistical support to the crew while they filmed in the region and transported all the cast and crew from base camp to the cliff-top sites. Nelson Helicopters offer a number of scenic flights within the region and offer a special *Lord of the Rings* location tour that flies over the *Chetwood Forest*, Mt Olympus and Mt Owen — it is highly recommended.

As members of the Fellowship cooked a meagre meal under the shelter of the rocks Merry and Pippin practised swordsmanship with Boromir. The keen eyes of Legolas spotted the approaching crebain and as the fire is hurriedly extinguished the Fellowship take cover to avoid detection.

Mt Olympus is appropriately named. The rocky outcrops sprout from the side of the mountain as if the gods themselves cast them there in some form of demented game. Over time, water has eroded away the softer rock to reveal a harder form, twisted and cracked into unbelievable columnar shapes. At times the valley below is covered in cloud and the stark pillars point to the sky in an accusing manner, adding to the mystical effect of this Olympian playground.

LOCATION	INTERNET
S40° 53.456'—E172° 30.654'	www.nelsonhelicopters.co.nz

Ian Brodie

New Line Productions

Above: A Nelson
Helicopters' Squirrel
perches on the only
flat ground.

Left: The keen eyes
of the Sindarin elf
Legolas spots the
approaching crebain.

Above: A crebain's
eye view of the area.

Right: The spot
where the
Fellowship hid from
the crebain.

Mt Owen *Dimrill Dale*

Ian Brodie

The 1800 m peak of Mt Owen is situated near Murchison, at the southern end of Kahurangi National Park. This park contains some of the oldest rocks in New Zealand and many geological features found here link the area with the ancient continent of Gondwanaland.

   As the helicopter crosses the eastern slopes of Mt Owen, a bleached moonscape of glaciated marble karst is exposed and as you move closer the scale of the rocks is revealed. The seemingly flat features are split with crevasses and interspersed with deep sinkholes like the face of a wrinkled troll — an area that truly displays the awesome power of nature. As water has fallen on the soft limestone over millions of years, a vast underground drainage network has evolved, resulting in New Zealand's largest cave system.

Mt Owen – some of the oldest rock formations in New Zealand.

LOCATION
S41° 33.493'—E172° 32.401'

Ian Brodie

Above: Surrealism in nature at Mt Owen.

Opposite above: Helicopter approach to Mt Owen.

Opposite below: Sam mourns the loss of Gandalf.

When you see this location for yourself, you start to realise the immensity of the huge undertaking in filming *The Lord of the Rings*. Totally exposed to the elements, crew and actors were transported here by helicopter for ten days to complete filming, and the results are spectacular.

To portray the depleted Fellowship escaping from the horrors of *Moria*, wooden steps were built on the site and the eastern doors of *Moria* added digitally. It is a tribute to the location scouts that one of the most emotively charged scenes in *The Fellowship of The Ring* was geographically enhanced by the bleached moonscape of Mt Owen.

While it's possible to tramp to this site, it's not recommended for other than experienced mountaineers, so sit back, relax and enjoy a magic helicopter ride.

Ian Brodie

New Line Production

87

The Southern Alps
The Misty Mountains

The Southern Alps form the backbone of the South Island. Stretching for over 550 km from Blenheim in the north to Fiordland in the south, they contain every peak in the country over 3000 metres.

Sandwiched between the Australian and Pacific tectonic plates, the mountains aren't static, with continual vertical and horizontal movement. Erosion caused by high rainfall and other factors have kept the mountains at a fairly stable height.

The alps have a considerable effect on South Island weather, and the predominant westerly winds create two distinct climates. Westerly fronts cause significant rainfall on the West Coast, but as they rise over the alps and drop their moisture, heating occurs. This creates a hot dry föhn wind in Canterbury and Otago, commonly called 'The Nor'wester'. The results are particularly noticeable when crossing the Main Divide — the western side of the alps is luxuriant bush and the east brown grass.

The Alps were the obvious choice to portray *The Misty Mountains* because of their height and similar climatic effects on the landscape.

As well as a number of generic locations, four specific sites were used in the trilogy. The northwestern slopes of Mt Earnslaw near Glenorchy portrayed *Caradhras* (Sindarin 'Redhorn') as the Fellowship attempted to cross *The Misty Mountains* via *The Redhorn Pass*. The alps in the Rangitata Region were where *Frodo* dropped the *One Ring*, which was picked up by *Boromir*.

Mt Aspiring and Mt Earnslaw were used in the spectacular opening sequence of *The Two Towers* to represent the high peaks around *Moria*, and the East Matukituki was used to show the Fellowship marching in single file through the snow. Both of these mountainous areas are accessible by helicopter with Heliworks on one of their Middle-earth tours (see page 125).

Opposite above:
Mt Owen.
Ian Brodie

Opposite below:
Small crevasses reach deep into the mountain. Ian Brodie

Overleaf left:
Mountain tarn near Mt Aspiring. Ian Brodie

Overleaf right:
Mt Pluto, beside Mt Earnslaw, was used as Zirak-zigil, where Gandalf finally smote the Balrog. Ian Brodie

The Misty Mountains were raised in the First Age. Stretching some 900 miles they contained the highest peaks in Middle-earth, Methedras (near Isengard), Caradhras (near Moria) and Zirak-zigil (where Gandalf smote the Balrog). Cloud and weather conditions caused by westerly winds gave rise to their name.

Erewhon — an introduction

Pierre Vinet

Above: The Riders of Rohan depart their capital, Edoras.

Below: Mt Sunday appears in the distant centre.

'Never shall I forget the utter loneliness of the prospect — only the little far away homestead giving sign of human handiwork, the vastness of mountain and plain, of river and sky; the marvellous atmospheric affects — sometimes black mountains against a white sky, and then again, after cold weather, white mountains against a black sky.' Thus wrote Samuel Butler in his classic novel *Erewhon*, a fine description of a harsh landscape that for eleven months became *Edoras*, the capital city of *Rohan*. Situated in a large mountain valley, the treeless golden tussock land of *Erewhon*, with its shingle-sloped alpine peaks providing a jagged backdrop, is a lonely prospect.

The closest town is Methven, 85 km to the northeast on the edge of the Canterbury Plains. In summer the town basks in 30°C heat caused by the hot northwest wind, playground for Cantabrians who jet boat the nearby rivers and picnic in the shade. In winter skiers occupy the many lodges, frequent the local bars and ski nearby Mt Hutt, one of New Zealand's finest fields. The cast and crew stayed here during filming and enjoyed the local hospitality.

Leaving Methven the road runs parallel to the Southern Alps across broad plains before reaching Mt Somers. The journey to Mt Sunday (*Edoras*) takes you through rural, exposed land where weather conditions are highly changeable. The alpine altitude means the area can experience extreme weather and temperature changes. An essential information sheet is available at local information offices and petrol stations. Make a right turn here, and the unpaved road passes through the Ashburton Gorge and skirts the clear trout-stocked Lakes Camp and Clearwater, before climbing steadily to a view that takes your breath away as *Erewhon* is revealed.

INTERNET
www.ChristchurchNZ.net

Ian Brodie

Mt Potts Station *Edoras*

Born high up in the spectacular Southern Alps, the Rangitata River is created by snow-fed tributaries and forms an alluvial shingle fan, with an associated large valley, virtually surrounded by towering mountains. Within this basin the terminal moraine of ancient glaciers have created rocky outcrops that seem to sprout from the shingle. One of these, Mt Sunday, was used to create *Edoras* and *Meduseld, King Theoden*'s hall, in Tolkien's realm of *Rohan*, the land of fabled horses and valiant warriors.

Descending into the Rangitata Valley Mt Sunday can be seen straight ahead, surrounded by brown tussock and tributaries of the braided river. There is no access to the mountain itself and the best views are obtained on the unpaved road as it passes the entrance to Mt Potts Station.

One of the more elaborate sets, *Edoras*, took eleven months to complete and created great interest with many Cantabrians who, armed with binoculars and cameras, travelled in over the weekends to catch a glimpse of the magnificent edifice. A cheeky newspaper journalist hired a light aircraft to fly over the area, obtaining a photographic scoop, with the images published worldwide.

Mt Potts is a high country station of 2700 ha and stretches from an altitude of 500 m to 2300 m. Approximately 70% is summer hill country and home to hardy New Zealand merino sheep. Accommodation in an alpine lodge or cottages on the station provides the perfect opportunity to experience life in the high country with a restaurant providing delicious home-cooked meals after a day of tramping, fishing or just quietly reading a book.

Pierre Vinet

The remaining members of the Fellowship arrive at Edoras.

Edoras (the Courts) was the capital of Rohan and comprised a number of dwellings encircling a central hill housing the King's hall, Meduseld. The roof and pillars of Meduseld were covered with pure gold, and it was also known as the Golden Hall of Edoras. Completed in 2569 (TA), it lay at the feet of the White Mountains near the River Snowbourn.

INTERNET	VIEWPOINT OF *EDORAS:* S43° 34.852'—E170° 58.212'
www.mtpotts.co.nz	*EDORAS:* S43° 32.899'—E170° 53.591'

Above: Aragorn looks across the valley to Helm's Deep which was digitally implanted into the Rangitata Valley landscape near Erewhon.

Right: A mountain stream near Edoras.

The Mackenzie Country —
an introduction

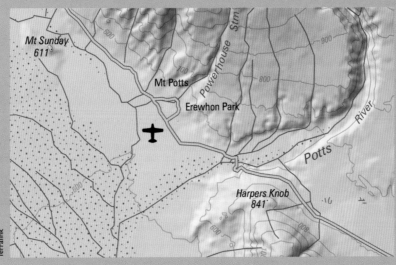

Pierre Vinet

Above: Meduseld had been standing for 450 years by the time of the War of the Ring.

Opposite above: The Pelennor Fields with the snow-capped Ered Nimrais in the background.

Ian Brodie

Opposite below: Lake Pukaki in sunshine, showing its unique opacity.

Ian Brodie

Passing over the 670 m Burkes Pass from Fairlie in the north into the Mackenzie Basin, the traveller will notice an immediate geographical change — from ordered farmland to brown tussock. Within this basin is New Zealand's highest mountain (Aoraki / Mt Cook 3762.9 m) and longest glacier (Tasman), which both contrast dramatically with the flat grass plains which lap up to the alps like a brown sea.

The area was named after a notorious Scotsman (James McKenzie) who was caught in the region with a large number of allegedly stolen sheep in the mid 1800s. His conviction, escape and subsequent pardon has become a local legend.

Travelling south across the tussock plains, the first view of the milky turquoise-blue Lake Tekapo is astounding. Its colour is derived from ground glacial rock suspended in the water. The small Church of the Good Shepherd on the lakefront is worthy of a visit and the vista from the tiny interior over the pulpit of lake and mountains is well photographed. Scenic flights over the alps are available from the nearby airport and there is a good range of accommodation and eating places in the village.

Leaving Tekapo the road continues towards Lake Pukaki, crossing large man-made canals constructed over thirty years ago to create New Zealand's largest hydroelectric power scheme. Utilising three natural and two man-made lakes, the Upper Waitaki scheme is a significant electricity source.

A tourist road starts beside one canal, ten minutes from Tekapo. This route will take you past a salmon farm (with a shop supplying fresh fish) as well as providing spectacular views of Mt Cook.

It rejoins the main road beside Lake Pukaki, another aquatic gem amongst the tussock. A further ten minutes' drive will bring you to the Mt Cook turnoff with the road leading straight ahead to the township of Twizel and the grassy plains of the *Pelennor Fields*.

The Mackenzie Country

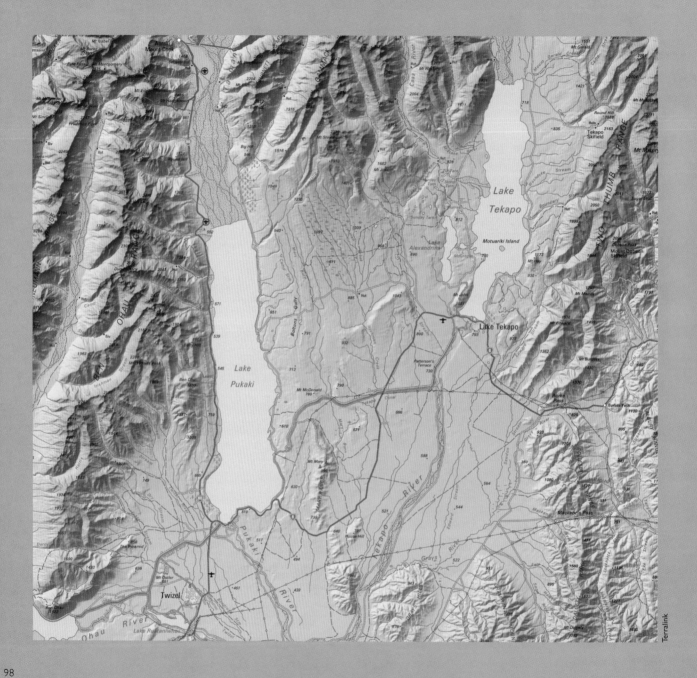

Mt Cook and Twizel

Before visiting Twizel, take the drive up to the alpine village of The Hermitage, just 106 km from Tekapo and nestled beneath the Southern Alps in Mount Cook National Park.

Mt Cook is surrounded by the highest peaks in New Zealand. Named Aoraki (Cloud in the sky) by Maori, it was first climbed on Christmas Day 1894 by three Christchurch men. The steep slopes still provide a challenge and were a training ground for world-famous New Zealand mountaineer, Sir Edmund Hillary, prior to his ascent of Mt Everest.

From The Hermitage there are a number of alpine walks with wonderful views. A highlight is a scenic ski-plane flight from the local airport taking you over the mountains for a snow landing high on the neve of the Tasman Glacier. If time is limited, one of the best walks is through the Hooker Flats. Allow four hours return to amble through bush on a well-formed track to Sefton Stream, with a view of the Hooker Glacier's terminal moraine.

To stay at The Hermitage is a real treat with magnificent lodgings surrounded by the *Ered Nimrais*. Nearby Glentanner Park also has accommodation or you can return to Twizel.

Named after Twizel Bridge in Northumberland, the town was built to house thousands of workers who descended on the area in the 1970s to construct the Upper Waitaki Power Scheme. The majority have since gone but the town is now a popular holiday destination, with nearby Lake Ohau and its ski-field. Close by is the man-made Lake Ruataniwha, which yields both rainbow and brown trout.

Snuggled under the foothills of the Southern Alps, the area is one of extreme weather conditions, as snow cloaks the area in winter whilst hot 'Nor'westers' in the summer can bring temperatures of over 30°C.

There is wide variety of accommodation and restaurants available in town as well as a well-equipped camping ground and numerous farm home-stays.

Aoraki (Mt Cook) from the Hermitage.

Ian Brodie

Twizel *the Pelennor Fields*

Ian Brodie

Pierre Vinet

Above top: Gandalf and Pippin crossed this small stream near Twizel en route to Minas Tirith.

Above: Cavalry charge at the Battle of the Pelennor Fields with the Ered Nimrais behind.

The largest battle scene filmed in the *Lord of the Rings* trilogy was the *Battle of the Pelennor Fields*. The area around Twizel provided the perfect ingredients: the *Ered Nimrais* (a snow-covered mountain chain); grassy fields; a remote location (with no sign of habitation); and a town nearby to provide the necessary infrastructure and amenities.

Most of the town was employed on the film and for over a month it was an amusing scene in the local bars every night as the combatants (still with remnants of make-up on their faces) discussed the day's attacks over a beer.

Tours are available to the location of the *Pelennor Fields* from Twizel and can be booked from the local Visitor Information Centre. As the location is on private land, this is the only means of access. The tour is much more than just a visit to some hills, however. Your guide will probably be a *Rohirrim* or *Gondorian Rider* or even a vicious Orc. As well as your guide explaining the intricacies of filming over 200 horses in majestic battle scenes, you will also be given an informative and highly interesting insight into high-country farming and the difficulties of working in such a harsh environment. The tour is highly recommended.

Ian Brodie

New Line Productions

Above: The mountain range to the right of Minas Tirith was shot just below the Hermitage at Mt Cook, looking southwest from the road leading up to the Hermitage. The mountain behind Minas Tirith is a different part of the Hooker Valley.

Left: Gandalf with the digital Minas Tirith in place.

The West Coast — an introduction

Top: A Nazgûl over the Dead Marshes.

Above: West Coast mountains.

The West Coast of the South Island is a region of verdant native bush, deep blue lakes, clear streams and snow-capped peaks. Receiving much more rainfall than its eastern neighbour, the consequent growth has resulted in a region of luxuriant trees and bush.

Known by New Zealanders simply as 'The Coast', this narrow province sandwiched between the Southern Alps and the Tasman Sea had its fair share of lawlessness during the mid 1800s, when miners descended on the area to harvest rich alluvial gold deposits from its many rivers.

Today tourism is a major industry and the West Coast Road, which stretches over 400 km from Haast in the south to Westport, provides the perfect alternative route north for those who may have travelled south down the eastern coast via *Edoras*.

Leaving Lake Wanaka the road skirts Lake Hawea before climbing over the 563.9 m Haast Pass to the coastal village of Haast. The nearby Haast Swamp was used as a landscape reference for *The Dead Marshes*.

Further north another popular stop is the Salmon Farm and restaurant near Lake Paringa which serves 'salmon everything'.

The road cuts a swathe through native trees and bush as it pushes north and there are some wonderful views of the Southern Alps as you arrive at the village of Fox Glacier. A DOC Information Centre provides details on the drive towards the base of the glacier and the many walks which are available.

From here the road winds over the Cook Saddle for a further 25 km to Franz Josef Glacier.

Franz Josef Glacier
the lighting of the beacons

When Peter Jackson sought a location to portray the *Lighting of the Beacons* he initially settled on a mountaintop near Queenstown. Unfortunately, filming was scheduled for the middle of the Central Otago summer and coincided with a total fire ban in the area. While searching the West Coast, he was shown photos of Mt Gunn and immediately settled on the location, which proved better than the original.

A drive up the access road takes you through the bush for wonderful views of the base of the glacier. It is an unusual sight — the glacier plunges down almost to the bush-line, with glaciers this low rarely seen outside arctic regions.

The best view of Mt Gunn is by helicopter. Local company Fox and Franz Heliservices did all the flying for this scene and know the area well. Based at Franz Josef and Fox Glaciers they offer tours over the location as well as scenic flights, including a landing on the glaciers.

Heliservices

Heliservices

Mt Gunn near Franz Josef.

The Ered Nimrais (Sindarin 'The White Mountains') ran east to west through Gondor and Rohan. As a means of communication, seven peaks on the eastern slopes had stores of firewood kept on their tops. The lighting of the beacons proved a swift means of communication in times of need.

INTERNET
www.scenic-flights.co.nz

Tarras *the flight to the ford*

Pierre Vinet

Above: Arwen and Frodo flee the Nazgûl.

Opposite: The Great East Road stretching through the pines.

Ian Brodie

The Great East Road is a lonely road to travel. During the Third Age Dwarves mainly used it as they travelled from the Misty Mountains to their mines in the Blue Mountains. Stretching from Rivendell in the East to Lindon and the Grey Havens in the West, the road was the only course available to Arwen as she rushed Frodo towards the Ford of Bruinen and the relative safety of Rivendell.

Tarras is a small farming village situated at the southern end of the Lindis Pass (970.4 m) linking the Mackenzie Basin with Central Otago. The Lindis Pass follows a Maori trail used by the Ngai Tahu, who travelled from the Waitaki River Basin to Lakes Wanaka and Hawea for summer fishing. John Turnbull Thomson found the trail in 1857 and in 1871 the brown hills became home to the first red deer liberated in Otago. An area of stark beauty, it is particularly photogenic in the late evening, as the setting sun turns the hills into distinct shades of brown.

In Tarras you'll find a general store, petrol station, souvenir shop, bookshop and a coffee shop, which is a great place to stop for a while. The Tarras area also offers the opportunity to stay on a merino sheep farm, an interesting alternative to a hotel or motel.

The *Great East Road* is a ten-minute drive away. Although the scenes from *The Fellowship of the Ring* were filmed on private land, much can still be seen from the road. Travel south towards Cromwell for approximately 6 km then turn right onto the unsealed Maori Point Road. After travelling a further 2 km you'll be in the area used as the *Great East Road* and to portray the *Flight to the Ford*, with filming carried out through the pine forests.

Continuing along Maori Point Road it's possible to take some excellent shots of the Southern Alps, used as the *Misty Mountains* surrounding *Rivendell*. The Clutha River can also be glimpsed to the left of the road. The largest river in New Zealand, it's slightly shorter than the Waikato River in the North Island but discharges almost twice the volume of water. The Maori name for the Clutha is Mata-au, which means surface current. The river was named by Scottish settlers after the Clyde River in Scotland (Clutha being Gaelic for Clyde) and proved to be a rich source of gold. At the beginning of the twentieth century over 150 dredges worked the river.

Wanaka *south of Rivendell/ Misty Mountains*

New Line Productions

Ian Brodie

Above top: Ancient ruins in the rough country south of Rivendell.

Above: The same hill with the Matukituki Valley in the background.

Lake Wanaka is a pleasant stopover, where the forced perspective room in Stuart Landsborough's Puzzling World & Great Maze allows you to experience how point of view scenes were filmed in the trilogy. At Wanaka Airport, visit the NZ Fighter Pilots Museum, try a Tandem Skydive with the company Orlando Bloom used, take a *Lord of the Rings* location flight with Wanaka Flightseeing, fire a bow at Have A Shot. Wanaka Sightseeing operates tours to many of the movie locations in the southern lakes area. When the cast and crew stayed in Wanaka during filming in 1999 it coincided with a serious flood after very heavy rain and they helped sandbag the town whilst they were there.

From the waterfront in town, look towards the Alps at the end of the lake and you'll see the backdrop used for *Gandalf*'s flight to *Rohan* with *Gwaihir*, after his rescue from *Orthanc*.

Another location is on the road marked Glendhu Bay and Treble Cone Ski Field. After approximately 15 km you pass Glendhu Bay on your right. Continue towards Treble Cone and just before the ski field turn-off you'll reach a view of the location. On the large brown hill on your right a ruined structure was digitally imposed and used in an aerial sequence, as the Fellowship headed south.

Returning to Wanaka, take State Highway 89 to Queenstown. The road soon starts to climb through the Cardrona Valley. Near the entrance to the Cardrona Ski Field and Waiorau Snow Farm stands the Cardrona Hotel, one of New Zealand's oldest.

Following the Cardrona River, the road climbs steadily towards the 1119.7 m summit where you can park your car and explore.

INTERNET	VIEWPOINT OF HILL WITH DIGITALLY ADDED RUINS
www.lakewanaka.co.nz	S44° 39.213'—E168° 58.342'

Crown Range route to Queenstown

Top: The Crown Range route.

Left: Tarras and the Great East Road region.

Motatapu

775.

Diamond
Lake

Paddock Bay

442.

Parkins
Bay

River

782

Glendhu
Bay

Glendhu Bay

Ian Brodie

Pierre Vinet

The view is expansive; to the left are the *River Anduin* and the *Pillars of the Argonath*, and high in the hills (straight ahead) is the *Dimrill Dale*. Now travel downhill another kilometre and make another stop. To the right is the *Ford of Bruinen* and in the far distance *Amon Hen* can be seen, nestled on the shore of *Nen Hithoel*. This area was also used for publicity stills of the Fellowship as they headed south in the rough country of *Eregion*.

INTERNET
www.wanakasightseeing.co.nz

Ian Brodie

'The road goes ever on' in a series of tight curves, before reaching a shelf of rich farmland with brownhills frowning on the right. There is another steep, downward spiral and six hairpin turns to negotiate to reach the valley floor. Turn left for a short drive to the *Pillars of the Kings*, a glass of fine Central Otago wine and the opportunity to throw oneself off a bridge into the *River Anduin* — attached to a bungy, of course!

After 5 km the Kawarau River is crossed, and immediately on your left is the headquarters of A.J. Hackett Bungy. An adventure born in Vanuatu and developed in New Zealand, bungy jumping has spread to all corners of the world. A.J. Hackett and speed skier, Henry Van Asch, developed the idea of jumping from a great height with an elastic bungy cord attached to their legs after watching videos of experiments by the Oxford University Dangerous Sports Club. In 1987 Hackett's jump from the Eiffel Tower created tremendous interest (and notoriety) for the new sport. In November 1988, the historic Kawarau Suspension Bridge became the world's first 'bungy bridge'. There are now six different bungy sites to jump from in the Queenstown area, including the 134-m high Nevis Highwire, which Orlando Bloom and crew tried out when they worked in the region.

Ian Brodie

Kawarau River *Pillars of the Kings*

Ian Brodie

Immediately opposite A.J. Hackett's bungy jump is the entrance road to Chard Farm Vineyard and a spectacular view of the *Anduin* and *Argonath* (*Sindarin 'Pillars of the Kings'*). Although the Pillars were computer-generated into each side of the river, the area is instantly recognisable.

Continuing along this short road you come to one of the founding vineyards in Central Otago. At latitude 45° South, Central Otago is perched on the southern edge of the grape-growing world. The northern hemisphere equivalent would run from Bordeaux to Southern Spain.

Chard Farm was established in 1987 and was one of the first commercial vineyards in the Southern Lakes District. Since then the area has become one of the biggest wine producers in New Zealand, with four sub-regions. The altitude and climate have distinct characteristics — you'll find New Zealand's highest vineyard above sea-level and the furthest vineyard from the sea. The continental climate gives warm, dry summers, cool autumns and cold winters, with relatively low humidity. The large diurnal temperature range helps seal in flavours and acids in white wines and encourages colour development in Pinot Noir. Cellar door sales at Chard Farm are available seven days from 10 a.m. to 5 p.m. Winery tours are by appointment only.

A further 2 km towards Cromwell you'll find Gibbston Valley Wines, boasting a popular restaurant, an adjacent cheese factory, and a unique and innovative wine cave. Dug 76 m into the Central Otago schist, tours are available daily between 10 a.m. and 4 p.m. Each tour culminates in the cave, where both Gibbston Valley Chardonnay and Pinot Noir can be tasted and enjoyed in unique surroundings.

The two huge carved likenesses of Isildur and Anárion in the chasm of the Anduin were built during the Third Age by Rómendacil of Gondor to mark the northern entrance to that realm.

Above: The Fellowship rafted from the bungy bridge.

Overleaf: Kawarau River with Chard farm middle centre.

Ian Brodie

PILLARS OF THE KINGS
S 45° 00.711'—E 168° 53.567'

The chance to raft down the *Anduin* is certainly an opportunity not to be missed and comes highly recommended. Local company Extreme Green Rafting worked with Peter Jackson for two years, providing all the rafting equipment and expertise for the river sequences. They now offer two trips down the *Anduin*: one includes some action-packed rafting, the other is a 'softer' option, which doesn't require wetsuits, for the less adventurous. Both trips float you past the location of the *Argonath*. Reservations can be made by calling their office in nearby Queenstown and transfers are provided from the town centre.

The Kawarau River flows from its source at Lake Wakatipu to Cromwell, where it joins the Clutha River at Lake Dunstan. The Kawarau Gorge was once a rich source of gold and you can see and experience how the miners of olden days lived at the Goldfields Mining Centre, a further 15 km towards Cromwell. Here you can take a guided tour of the diggings and an exhilarating jet-boat ride down the river.

Back on the road towards Queenstown and approximately 1 km past the Crown Range exit, turn right towards Arrowtown and the *Ford of Bruinen*.

The small Elven boats approach the Argonath on the River Anduin.

With a length of over 1300 miles, the River Anduin is the longest in Middle-earth. From Mirkwood in the north to Gondor in the south, it flowed past many regions before finally spreading out into a broad delta and entering the sea through the Ethir Anduin, south of Dol Amroth. The Fellowship spent eleven days paddling downstream from Lothlórien, covering a distance of almost 300 miles to the breaking of the Fellowship at Amon Hen.

INTERNET
www.extremegreenrafting.com

113

Arrowtown *the Ford of Bruinen*

Destination Queenstown

Destination Queenstown

Located a scenic twenty-minute drive from Queenstown, Arrowtown promotes itself as 'Born of Gold'. In 1862 William Fox discovered one of the world's richest gold-bearing areas here, and in the ensuing gold rush over 7000 Europeans and Chinese came seeking alluvial gold in the nearby Arrow and Shotover Rivers. The bustling community had its share of lawlessness and notorious gangsters and thugs descended on the gold fields to make a living by various nefarious means. The excellent Lakes District Centennial Museum situated on the narrow one-way main street provides a wealth of information about the area, including the many characters who worked the gold fields.

Here autumn is especially wonderful; the tree-lined main street becomes a leafy carpet of red and gold as smoke from the chimneys of the original miners' cottages creates a hazy atmosphere in shafts of sunlight. Larches interspersed with pines on the nearby hills create golden pools of colour and the air is clear and crisp with the crackle of frost in the morning confirming another breathtaking day. Many of Arrowtown's shops and galleries feature the work of local artists, so take your time to browse and don't forget your camera.

Restored Chinese miners' cottages can be viewed via a short walk from the main street, an interesting reminder of Arrowtown's past.

Nearby the world-famous Millbrook Resort features luxurious accommodation and restaurants surrounded by a par-72 world championship golf course, designed by Sir Bob Charles, New Zealand's renowned master golfer.

Above top: Lake Hayes, near Queenstown.

Above: Miners' cottage near Arrowtown.

INTERNET
WWW.QUEENSTOWNNZ.CO.NZ

The *Ford* is only minutes from the centre of the village on the Arrow River. Park in the area behind the main street and walk down to the adjacent riverbank.

To reach the exact spot walk upstream for some 200 m, which can involve wading the river (normally only ankle deep). This will place you in the direction the *Nazgûl* charged as *Arwen* ferried *Frodo* across the river on *Asfaloth*, her Elven steed. The path the *Nazgûl* took down to the river is clearly visible on your left.

The scene showing the flooding of the river was filmed in the Shotover River at Skippers Canyon (see page 87). One of the more 'public' locations, during the three days spent filming here many locals lined the riverbank to watch. The local Saffron Restaurant became one of the cast's favourite dinner locations.

You can still fossick for gold here and stores on the main street hire pans to enable a search for gold and a means of recovering your holiday costs.

The magical flood *Arwen* invoked to dispel the *Nazgûl* had an eerie echo in reality, with a genuine flash flood washing away part of the set during filming of *The Fellowship of the Ring*.

> The Ford of Rivendell was located where the Great East Road crossed the River Bruinen (Sindarin 'Loudwater'). Under the power of Elrond it could be raised at will to stop any unwanted visitors and provided the last bastion of defence into the Hidden Valley.

Above: Paddle through the Arrow River to the Ford of Bruinen.

Left: The sight of the nine Nazgûl together would terrify the most stouthearted.

FORD OF RRUINEN
S 44° 56.147'—E 168° 49.863'

Arrowtown *The Gladden Fields*

Pierre Vinet

Above: From The Gladden Fields, the ring crossed the Misty Mountains twice on its journey back to Mordor.

Below: On a cold winter morning the Gladden Fields take on a foreboding atmosphere.

The *Gladden Fields* are only a short walk away. Amble down Buckingham Street past the delightfully restored miners' cottages and turn left into Nairn Street. Continuing down will take you to the wide expanse of Wilcox Green, where a path through the trees beside the river will take you into the location.

This scene was filmed in winter with the leafless trees adding to the sense of foreboding as *Isildur* was attacked by Orcs from the *Misty Mountains*. Deceived by *The One Ring* he was to lose his life and be taken by the waters of the *Anduin*.

Autumn is another wonderful time to visit when the river takes on a totally different perspective as many shades of gold both on the trees and underfoot combine to create a reflective hue that rivals *Lothlórien*.

Ian Brodie

The Gladden Fields (Sindarin 'Loeg Ningloron') were a series of marshy paddocks situated at the confluence of the Gladden and Anduin Rivers. An important geographical location in the story of The One Ring, it was here in 2(TA) that Isildur was ambushed by Orcs on his way to reclaim the Northern Kingdom of Arnor. Attempting to escape, The One Ring betrayed him when it slipped off his finger. In later years a group of Hobbits settled in the area eventually leading to the rediscovery of The One Ring by Déagol (cousin of Sméagol).

GLADDEN FIELDS
S44° 56.324' —E168° 50.327'

Skippers Canyon *the Ford of Bruinen*

New Line Productions

Returning to Queenstown, you'll see the Coronet Peak ski area on your right. Another sealed access road lies closer to Queenstown, designed to transport skiers in the winter but open all year, with an imposing view of the Wakatipu Basin from the car park.

Skiing and snowboarding are popular during winter and every year international visitors enjoy the spectacular conditions. There are five ski fields within 90 minutes of Queenstown.

The Coronet Peak road also provides access to Skippers Canyon. The preferred choice is to travel into the Canyon with local 4WD operator Nomad Safaris, who provide specialist Lord of the Rings Tours, with the added advantage that a number of their drivers took part in the filming. The Skippers Road is closed to rental cars and is tortuous in places, especially for drivers unfamiliar with these sorts of roads.

In its heyday, Skippers was the most prolific local gold field, with each square foot of its bed

Ian Brodie

said to hold an ounce of gold, and well worth a guided tour into the canyon. The steep valley walls, winding road, stark brown hills and contrasting snow-covered peaks are beautiful, but of equal interest is the river itself. The part close to the original bridge (approximately 12 km into the gorge) was used to portray the *Ford of Bruinen* in flood, one of the most dramatic scenes from *The Fellowship of the Ring*.

A little further towards Queenstown, you'll pass historic Gantleys Restaurant on your left. Their fine food and wines were enjoyed by the cast and crew, as it sits opposite the Quality Resort Alpine Lodge, used as 'wet weather cover' for interior shots.

Above top: Arwen turns to face the Nazgûl at the Ford of Bruinen.

Above: The same location today.

INTERNET
www.nomadsafaris.co.nz

Queenstown

Destination Queenstown

Queenstown with the Remarkables on the right.

Pierre Vinet

Queenstown is one of New Zealand's most well-known and popular tourist destinations. Nestled in an alpine valley alongside Lake Wakatipu, it's good enough for all the tourist clichés to ring true.

Maori legend tells of a tipua (demon) who seized a beautiful girl. Rescued by her lover while the demon slept, the hero set fire to the area and as the flames licked the demon's body he drew his knees upwards in pain. The enormous amount of fat in his body fanned the fire and a large chasm was dug as he writhed. Rain and snow extinguished the fire, but the demon was destroyed — all except for his heart. Today, the shape of the lake reveals his outline, while his beating heart causes the lake to rise and fall.

The first Europeans to settle in the area were William Gilbert Rees and Paul von Tunzelmann. Cutting their way through the thorny undergrowth for weeks on end they arrived at Lake Wakatipu and decided to go no further. They settled their sheep in the remoteness, not realising their peaceful existence was about to change with William Fox's discovery of gold in the Arrow River. The population exploded and Queenstown became the major service centre supplying the miners.

Tourism is now the 'goldmine' and visitors from around the world descend on Queenstown, also known as The Adventure Capital of New Zealand.

The cast and crew fell in love with the area, with the Hobbits also finding plenty of time to explore the nightclubs and hotels. With the local High School doubling as audition headquarters, schoolteachers became Orcs and taxi drivers were transformed into the people of *Rohan*. At the height of casting over 500 people a day queued for their opportunity to enter Middle-earth.

> I recalled sitting in Queenstown against the mountain range aptly titled the Remarkables and feeling I was actually living the books. It was like Tolkien had walked across New Zealand.
>
> SEAN ASTIN

The remote and lonely country encountered by the Fellowship.

With a permanent population of just 11,000, Queenstown now hosts over 1 million visitors a year. The main street, closed to traffic, is a mecca for those who like to sit in the sun and 'do coffee' with the imposing lake and mountain view offering a perfect backdrop. The sheer breadth of tourist activities is impossible to list but there is something for every taste and age, with a number of reservation offices offering excellent advice.

A trip on the grand old lady of the lake is a highlight. The steamer *Earnslaw* recently celebrated her ninetieth anniversary, having been assembled in 1912 to provide transportation from the railhead at Kingston. Just over 50 m in length and with a beam of 7.3 m, the stately steamer now operates a number of tourist excursions on Lake Wakatipu. The cruise to Walter Peak offers distant views of *Amon Hen* (Closeburn).

The ascent of Bob's Peak by gondola provides a breathtaking view. One of the steepest cableways in the world, it rises some 446 m over a distance of 731 m. There is a fully licensed restaurant at the top providing one of the most romantic viewpoints for dinner in the world.

Queenstown can be visited and enjoyed all year round, snow falling in the town in winter provides a white blanket to excite skiers, while summer temperatures reach over 30° Celsius.

Allocate at least three days here to fully appreciate the film locations. Also, take some time to visit the Rattlesnake Bar, The Cow Restaurant and Rydges Hotel, all used by the cast as watering holes.

Even though we are right down here at the bottom of the world we have mountains, forests and fields, rivers, lakes and waterfalls that have a familiar yet slightly fantastical appearance.

PETER JACKSON

Deer Park Heights

N

ARROWTOWN
LAKE HAYES

FRANKTON

REMARKABLES

CORONET PEAK

KAWARAU
RIVER

EAST SUMMIT
LOOKOUT

MT AURUM
FRANKTON ARM

④

MOVIE
SET

DEER
GOATS
SHEEP

①

MOUNTAIN
TARN

②

⑦

③

PICNIC AREA

⑥

⑤

WALKWAY

Location numbers on
pages 120 and 124
refer to this map.

WEST SUMMIT
LOOKOUT

Deer Park Heights

Deer Park Heights is off the main road to Te Anau and about twenty minutes' drive from Queenstown. After passing the airport entrance and crossing the Kawarau River, take the road on the right marked Kelvin Heights. The entrance is a further 5 km on your left.

Deer Park Heights is an 800-m conical hill and its top is one giant movie set with a number of walks revealing many locations, all with panoramic views. Looking north over the airport the *River Anduin* can be seen flowing towards the *Pillars of the Kings*. The hillside was used for locations in all three films and because of its proximity to Queenstown, it was utilised for many 'pick-up' shots.

All locations from the three films are marked with signs making them easy to find. These numbers are repeated on the map above.

Below: The mountain tarn (1) with The Remarkables in the background.

To find locations from *The Fellowship* and *The Return of the King* take the unpaved road to the top of the hill where you'll be confronted by a Korean prison used as a set in the 1986 film *The Rescue*. The first location is a track running a few metres to the left of the road by the prison, heading south, where *Gandalf* was photographed for publicity shots.

The second is a small mountain tarn 500 m south of the car park (1). Here a short sequence was filmed depicting *Gandalf* riding to *Minas Tirith* in the first film and with *Pippin* in the third and final film. Return to the car park and drive down the hill a little way. Just after crossing the cattle stop pull over to the left and you will see the exit wall from the *Paths of the Dead* (7).

Ian Brodie

MOUNTAIN TARN S45° 02.456'—E 168° 43.700'

PATHS OF THE DEAD: S45° 02.249—E168° 43.468' facing 266°

Ian Brodie

Chris Coad

Above: Deer Park Heights, where Gandalf the Grey walked.

Left: Rohirrim refugees flee Edoras.

Overleaf: An aerial view of Deer Park Heights. Ian Brodie

121

Deer Park Heights *The Two Towers*

Ian Brodie

Ian Brodie

Above top: The view Legolas had of the approaching Wargs. Today only the occasional goat can be seen.

Above: As Hama rode around this cliff face the Warg rider struck.

A number of scenes from *The Two Towers* were filmed here. It is interesting to note that the locations are sometimes quite far apart geographically but the finished sequences are a seamless action scene. Starting from the tollbooth at the foot of the hill drive up the hill and stop by the large gate on the left (3). Through here and down on the left is the large rock wall the *Warg* scout jumped off and killed *Hama*. Continue on up the hill and stop beside a small tarn on your right (2). Here *Gimli* was thrown from his runaway horse, to the amusement of *Éowyn*. A little further up the road is a walking trail to a site immediately recognizable as the cliff face *Aragorn* was dragged over (6). Below the cliff is more grass, not the expected precipice or river (that scene was filmed on the nearby Kawarau). This position was also where the *Wargs* and *Riders of Rohan* clashed. Across the road and a little way up this hill is where *Legolas* did his amazing jump onto his horse before battle (5). A little further on is the rock shelf where *Legolas* fired his first arrows at the *Wargs* as they came over the hill (5). The final location is the most dramatic. Around the large tarn near the top car park is where the *Rohirrim Refugees* were led on a perfectly clear and pristine winter morning (1).

The Remarkables *Dimrill Dale*

The movie sequence showing a depleted and demoralised Fellowship fleeing from their ordeal in the terrifying *Mines of Moria* without *Gandalf* was filmed in two locations at opposite ends of the South Island. After the Fellowship gathers their composure, *Aragorn* leads them down the steep slopes of the *Dimrill Dale* towards *Lothlórien*. This location is situated high in the Remarkables Ranges and can be reached by one of two different routes.

The energetic can drive to the top of the Remarkables Ski Field, which is situated 20 km from Queenstown. Upon reaching the car park the alpine tarn of Lake Alta is a further 20-minute hike up the hill. A reasonable level of fitness is required.

By far the easier option (and easily the more exciting) is to take a helicopter flight with local company Heliworks, who were responsible for providing helicopters and pilots for most of the aerial filming and transportation for the entire trilogy. Experts in their field, they now know this part of Middle-earth intimately, and their experienced pilots Alfie Speight and Dennis Egerton can transport you directly to the many locations centered around Queenstown.

The company offers three *Lord of the Rings* flights ranging from a 30-minute excursion to Lake Alta, *Amon Hen* and the *Ford of Bruinen* through to a 90-minute aerial extravaganza covering all the local locations. Flying like *Gwaihir* around the Southern Alps on your own Middle-earth adventure is a very special experience, and one that comes highly recommended as a climax to any tour of Middle-earth New Zealand.

Pierre Vinet

Ian Brodie

Above top: The depleted Fellowship flee the Dimrill Dale.

Above: Lake Alta.

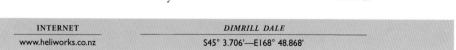

INTERNET	*DIMRILL DALE*
www.heliworks.co.nz	S45° 3.706'—E168° 48.868'

125

Ian Brodie

Pierre Vinet

Above top: Lake Alta after a snowfall.

Above: Aragorn crosses the River Silverlode.

Heliworks will fly you directly to a landing point high above this point and from here wonderful photographs can be obtained of the *Dimrill Dale* and *Celebrant*.

Lake Alta is a typical alpine tarn. In winter it's frozen and covered with snow while in summer hardy sun-baked alpine plants eke out a living from the sparse soil under the schist rock. Schist is a metamorphic rock common to the mountains of the South Island, and formed when rocks deep within the earth are affected by heat or great pressure. Akin to slate, it's crumbly by nature and can be easily split along its many bands. A popular building material, it clads many fine homes in the Southern Lakes region.

A deep valley extending from the western doorway of the Mines of Moria, the Dimrill Dale was known by the Dwarves as Azanulbizar and as Nanduhirion by the Elves. The door itself was more correctly called the Dimrill Gate. Descending steeply the path skirted the Mirrormere (Dwarvish 'Kheled-zâram'), one of the Dwarves' most sacred places. Legend told of Durin the Deathless looking into the still deep waters to see his head crowned by seven stars —— thus confirming his royalty. From its source in the Dimrill Dale, the Celebrant (Sindarin 'Silver-course' and also known as the Silverlode River) followed the valley and thence through Lothlórien.

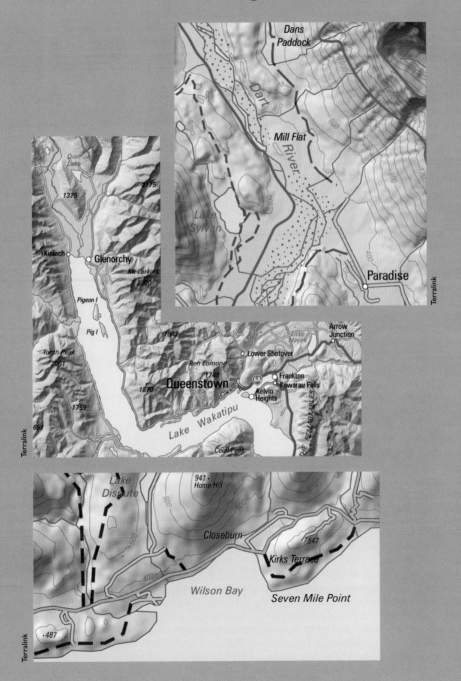

Dans
Paddock

Dart

Mill Flat

River

Lake
Sylvan

Paradise

Terralink

Diamond
Lake

1175

1375

Kinloch

Glenorchy

Mt Larkins
2300

Pigeon I

Pig I

Tooth Peak
2061

1870

1759

691

Terralink

1842

Lake
Hayes

Arrow
Junction

Lower Shotover

Ben Lomond
1748

Queenstown

6A

Frankton
Kawarau Falls

Kelvin
Heights

Lake Wakatipu

Cecil Peak

THE REMARKABLES

Lake
Dispute

941
Home Hill

600

Closeburn

547

Kirks Terrace

Wilson Bay

Seven Mile Point

400

600

487

Terralink

Closeburn *Amon Hen*

Pierre Vinet

Orcs approach
Amon Hen.

The drive to Glenorchy follows the shores of Lake Wakatipu for 45 km. At times the road climbs high bluffs with views of the lake and mountains, at others it passes secluded bays at lake-level. Pine trees cover the lower mountains in places and there are some lovely walkways. Have your fishing rod handy as brown and rainbow trout cruise close to the shore — Viggo Mortensen was spotted fly-fishing here, although remember to organise a fishing licence.

Closeburn is situated 8 km from Queenstown. While the actual location of *Amon Hen* is not accessible, a stop on the lakeshore is suggested, after descending the hill to Closeburn Bay. The area used for filming was set amongst the pine trees on the peninsula on your left, and the use of multiple sites to portray one scene is very apparent here. Filming for the climatic finale of *The Fellowship of the Ring* was undertaken at Closeburn, Paradise and Mavora Lakes, with the skill of the film-makers weaving all three places together seamlessly. In summer, Closeburn is an ideal barbecue area, very reminiscent of the scented forests of *Ithilien*. St John's wort and sweet briar roses send out their distinctive perfumes and their riot of colour contrasts superbly with the cream and white foxgloves.

Nearby Matakauri Lodge is the closest accommodation to Closeburn and Twelve Mile Delta, a totally secluded luxury lodge which makes for a wonderful place to stay.

The scent of pine trees and dramatic views of lake and mountains bring *Ithilien* and Middle-earth to mind, so it's little wonder that Twelve Mile Delta was used to portray the *Ithilien Camp*.

> Amon Hen (Sindarin 'The Hill of the Eye') was built by the men of Númenor as a watch-house to mark the northern border of Gondor. One of three tall hills on both sides of the Anduin and the Falls of Rauros, its companions were Amon Lhâw (Sindarin 'The Hill of the Ear') on the eastern bank and Tol Brandir (the Tindrock) in the middle of the river.

AMON HEN
S45° 03.562'—E168° 33.804'

128

Pierre Vinet

Situated 4 km past Closeburn is Twelve Mile Delta, with a large camping area and a number of walks and mountain bike tracks to take you into *Ithilien*. Two areas were used here to portray *Ithilien*, where *Sam* saw his *Oliphants*. To reach this location go down to the river and walk towards Lake Wakatipu. The bank on your right is where *Frodo*, *Sam* and *Sméagol* watched the battle between the men of *Harad* and the *Rangers of Gondor*. To reach the cliff top hiding space where *Sam* and *Sméagol* discussed the merits of cooking coneys with 'taters', return to the walking track at the western end of the river.

Above: Deep in thought, Faramir surveys Ithilien.

Overleaf: Mountain stream of Twelve Mile Delta.

Ian Brodie

Here Frodo and Sam rested after the horror of the Black Gate, and witnessed a fierce battle on the upper ridge and saw the legendary mûmak.

The people of Harad waged war against Gondor almost continuously during the Third Age. Their land lay to the south and was divided into a number of small fiefdoms, all eager to lay claim to Gondor. The dark-skinned men of Harad were adept warriors and used a number of techniques to attack, including mûmakil, pachyderms of immense size complete with war-towers on their backs.

RIVER-BED POINT OF VIEW CLIFF-TOP HIDING SPACE
S45° 04.008'—E168° 32.683'

 Ian Brodie

A general view of the area where Sméagol presented his coneys to the hobbits.

The track takes you across a footbridge spanning a deep chasm as Twelve Mile Stream rushes through on its way to Lake Wakatipu. Pause and look at the pool on your left — the perfect place to imagine *Sméagol* catching his favourite food. Walk along the track for approximately ten minutes and you'll find yourself in the area where *Sméagol* caught the coneys. You can also walk through the undergrowth to the cliff edge where the trio watched the battle. Don't get too close to the edge however, as there is a dangerous overhang. It is a lovely walk and in the spring and summer herbs and wildflowers bloom in abundance on both sides of the track. It is the perfect representation of *Ithilien* with the flowers combining with dry ground and tough matagouri bushes to create the illusion of a land slowly falling into decay under the evil influence of *Sauron*. The track continues up to the next plateau, with wonderful views of the lake and mountains.

CONEY COOKING WITH SMÉAGOL
S45° 04.151' —E168° 32.587'

Pierre Vinet

Ian Brodie

Above: Rangers of Ithilien in their distinctive camouflaged clothing.

Left: This area of the track just before the Twelve Mile Stream footbridge was where the Rangers of Ithilien ambushed the Men of Harad.

Glenorchy — an introduction

Ian Brodie

Dart River Jetboat Safaris

The little village of Glenorchy nestles at the northern end of Lake Wakatipu with the jagged peaks of the snow-capped *Misty Mountains* acting as a spectacular backdrop.

Maori passed through this area in their search for pounamu (jade or greenstone as it is known locally) but it wasn't until 1862 that settlers arrived, using the broad river flats for grazing. Some 3000 gold miners soon followed but yields proved less spectacular than in other regions, and they soon left. Tourism evolved in the 1890s and a number of guesthouses were built for adventurous European visitors travelling up the lake from Queenstown. The discovery of scheelite (used to make weapons grade tungsten) in 1905 saw over 50 workers extracting the ore until the 1980s. Today, Glenorchy has a population of just over 200 and has evolved into a centre for eco-tourism.

Glenorchy is also a gateway to Mt Aspiring National Park, covering 355,543 hectares and part of Te Wahipounamu (Southwest New Zealand World Heritage Area). A DOC information centre in the village provides information on the many outstanding walks that abound in the area.

Above top: Lake Wakatipu, at Kinloch.

Above: The stunning view of the Wizard's Vale on the road from Queenstown to Glenorchy.

Accommodation ranges from backpacker to luxury and the Glen Roydon Lodge provides good food and excellent accommodation at reasonable prices. It became the local hangout for the crew and the proprietor, Eileen Todd, speaks proudly of her morning coffee with Peter Jackson and her time on the set of *Amon Hen*.

A couple of days can easily be spent in the area, walking, jet boating and horse trekking to *Isengard*, *Amon Hen* and *Lothlórien*.

Above: Saruman's army depart Isengard.

Left: The snow-clad slopes of Mt Earnslaw.

Overleaf: Glenorchy with Mt Alfred distant centre and Mt Earnslaw distant right.
Ian Brodie

Glenorchy *Isengard and Lothlórien*

Right: The Tower of Orthanc nestled in Nan Curunír.

Opposite above: Mt Earnslaw. Ian Brodie

Opposite below: The same area in winter, used for the opening scene in *The Two Towers*.

Ian Brodie

New Line Productions

Leaving the village going north take the road marked Paradise. After a while the magnificent Arcadia guesthouse (now a private home) appears on your left. Continuing on, the river flats give way to patches of beech forest. There is some confusion as to how the name Paradise came about, some say it was named after the Paradise Ducks in the area, others because of its beautiful location.

The Wizard's Vale (Nan Curunír) was a large, almost encircled, valley at the southern end of the Misty Mountains. The peak of Methedras (Sindarin 'Last Peak') lay to the north with the smaller mountain of Dol Baran to the west. Holding a strategically advantageous position, the Vale looked over the Gap of Rohan and Fords of Isen, effectively guarding passage of any troops making their way from East to West. Helm's Deep was approximately 100 km from Isengard.

After 26 km, Dan's Paddock is reached. The area up the slopes on your right (where paddock and forest meet) was where *Gandalf* rode up to *Isengard*.

The high peak of Mt Earnslaw towering down on the paddock was also used to portray part of *The Misty Mountains*.

Travel another 2 km though beautiful forest and open paddocks and just after leaving a clearing to enter a forest glade, make another stop. Here the edge of the forest was used to portray the Fellowship entering *Lothlórien*.

Past this point the terrain becomes rough, with small streams to be forded. The preferred option is an excursion with Dart River Safaris and Dart Stables. The guides themselves are a special part of the journey — many worked on the film and have interesting experiences to relate.

DAN'S PADDOCK: S44° 40.417'—E 168° 20.457'
EDGE OF LOTHLÓRIEN: S44° 39.442'—E168° 20.100'

Above: The
legendary Oliphants.

Right: Sam, Frodo
and Sméagol watch
their progress.

Dart River Safaris and Funyaks
Isengard, Lothlórien and Amon Hen

Dart River Jetboat Safaris

Left: A Dart River Safaris' jet boat thunders down the Dart.

Below: The golden eaves of Lothlórien.

Glenorchy-based Dart River Safaris operate tours into the Dart River Valley by jet boat and funyak canoe, providing an ideal opportunity to explore *Isengard, Lothlórien* and *Amon Hen*. They also provide transfers from Queenstown.

The adventure starts with a 45-minute back-road journey into the depths of the mountains. Passing *Isengard*, several stops are made before a 20-minute bush walk to the jet boat. This area has a magical quality — reminiscent of the *Old Forest* or *Mirkwood the Great*, the trees appear to have a permanence of thousands of years. To complete the scene small rivulets of water trickle through the mossy walls with the only other sound that of the Dart River rushing over sandy gravel.

All this is merely an entrée for the exciting 90-minute jet-boat ride. Heading further up river initially, the surrounding mountains envelop you as you skim over the narrow shallows. Frequent stops are made and your driver will demonstrate the jet boat's capability, including the famous 'Hamilton Turn'. Returning to Glenorchy, the river broadens into many braids and a stop is made close to the area of bush portrayed as *Amon Hen* where *Merry* and *Pippin* were captured by Orcs.

Pierre Vinet

INTERNET
www.dartriverjet.co.nz

Dart Stables *Amon Hen and Lothlórien*

Right: The proud Boromir, son of Denethor II meets his doom at Amon Hen.

Opposite: Paradise on earth — on a Dart Stables' overnight horse trek.

Ian Brodie

Pierre Vinet

One of the most magical adventures in the area is a horse trek with Dart Stables. From Glenorchy there are options to suit both novice and experienced riders, including the highly recommended two-day trek, which passes by two film locations, taking you close to *Lothlórien* and the hillside of *Amon Hen*.

Here at the edge of Lothlórien, relieved at their escape from Moria but filled with sorrow at the death of Gandalf, the Fellowship are met and taken to Galadriel. A short walk through the bush nearby is Amon Hen where Boromir finally succumbed to Lurtz, before the huge Orc met his own end at the hand of Aragorn.

Trotting along beside the river, the path takes you closer to the mountains before entering the primeval beech forest. The destination for the night is a well-maintained hut in a clearing surrounded by a patch of beautiful native bush, shown in the movie as the site where the Fellowship are met by *Haldir* and taken to *Galadriel*.

This area is one of the most exquisite locations in New Zealand. Dappled sunlight filters through the trees illuminating the luxuriant moss underfoot and dry leaves gather in drifts in every undulation. It is the perfect vision of *Lothlórien*.

After dinner by candlelight there is time to relax and experience an invigorating splash in the waterfall plunge pool. Sitting under the stars beside the roaring open fire the transportation to Middle-earth is complete and it would come as no surprise if *Gildor Inglorion* and his Elven kindred quietly joined you for food and drink.

INTERNET
www.glenorchy.co.nz

The Routeburn Track Road *Isengard*

Ian Brodie

The Routeburn Track Road will take you to the best view of the location where Weta Studios worked their amazing digital magic to add in the visually stunning tower and pits of *Isengard*. Departing Glenorchy, initially take the Glenorchy/Paradise Road before turning left onto the road marked Kinloch and Routeburn. After crossing the Dart River turn immediately right and travel 2 km — the best view is obtained some 100 m after crossing Scott Creek.

Standing by the paddock one can easily imagine *Isengard* nestled into *Nan Curunír* (the Wizard's Vale) with the mighty peak of *Methedras* towering over the valley. Real landscapes and digital effects have been combined here with great effectiveness. Initially, a helicopter with a large 'Spacecam' camera mounted underneath was flown in precise circles around the area, gathering the required landscape images. Then the miniature *Orthanc* was added and a series of bush-covered hills filmed many miles away on the West Coast were added (to the left of the circle). Finally the Dart River was removed and after hundreds of hours of digital work, the whole area was created.

The viewpoint near Scott Creek looks into the Wizard's Vale.

A fortress built by the Dúnedain of Gondor at the height of their power, the Ring of Isengard contained the Tower of Orthanc (Sindarin 'Forked Height'), built of an unbreakable black rock and rising 500 feet above the plain. Deserted during the Third Age by the men of Gondor, it was reoccupied by Saruman the White, who destroyed the lush gardens and had it fortified. Underneath the ring he built many armouries and pits to house his countless armies of Orcs. The Ents destroyed Isengard during the War of the Ring but the tower survived because of its impregnable rock, and was retaken by Gondor in the Fourth Age.

If you really want to savour the area, there is also the opportunity to camp here. Continue on and take the Lake Sylvan Road on your right. At the end is a DOC Camping Ground, which makes a perfect overnight stop with the added advantage of undertaking the walk to Lake Sylvan itself. Taking just over an hour to reach the bush-fringed lake, the track is a delight in itself, with moss-covered trees reminiscent of *Fangorn Forest* providing a home to many species of native birds.

VIEW OF THE WIZARD'S VALE
S44° 45.433' —E168° 18.963'

Walking tracks

In the Glenorchy area there are a number of excellent tramps and walks which allow you to really enter into the isolation and majesty that is Middle-earth Aotearoa. Mountain peaks, rushing streams, brown tussock and green bush all combine to provide a perfect reproduction of the *Eregion* region of Middle-earth. So grab a staff, a backpack and some good food and undertake your own adventure through the wilds.

A very good base is Kinloch Lodge; family-run accommodation set on the shores of Lake Wakatipu. With no television or cellphone coverage a couple of nights spent here are a pure tonic. Rates are very reasonable and options range from self-catering hostelry style through to the Heritage Rooms, which include dinner, bed and breakfast.

Ian Brodie

The Routeburn Track provides an escape into Eregion.

One of the more popular walks is the Routeburn Track, which is a three-day tramp from near Kinloch across the Harris Saddle (1279 m) to the Milford Road.

Kinloch Lodge is also a good starting point for two other tramps, both starting nearby. The Greenstone Track is an easy 2-3 day (37 km) tramp from Greenstone Station following the Greenstone River to Lake McKellar and then on to the Milford Road.

The Caples Track starts and ends off the Greenstone and is a moderate 2-3 day climb over 23 km. Both tracks can be combined to make a five-day exploration of one of the most beautiful parts of New Zealand.

These three walks can also be undertaken as guided tramps. Led by professionals, this is a great way to learn about the many aspects of New Zealand's natural heritage.

Eregion (Sindarin 'Land-of-Holly') nestled against the western side of the Misty Mountains south of Rivendell. Settled by the Noldorin elves in 750 (SA), it was here that the Rings of Power were forged. Led by Celebrimbor (a descendent of Fëanor) many other beautiful crafts were made as the Elves worked in harmony with the Dwarves of Moria. In the end, only 750 years later, all was destroyed by Sauron the Deceiver as he secretly forged The One Ring to control all others.

INTERNET
www.kinlochlodge.co.nz

Queenstown day tour

Elven princesses in the ethereal light of Lothlórien.

Leaving Queenstown take the main route to Arrowtown passing Arthur's Point and one of the oldest hotels in New Zealand. The road then crosses the Edith Cavel Bridge, where below on the left is the departure point for the Shotover Jet. Operating high-powered jet boats down the river, they offer a spectacular ride.

In Arrowtown, a welcome coffee stop before the Cromwell road, take the road down to the Arrow River to view the *Ford of Bruinen* and continue on to the *Gladden Fields*. At the main State Highway turn left and drive for 5 km before crossing the Kawarau River Bridge, where the entrance road to Chard Farm is on your right. A short distance up this road the *River Anduin* and location of the *Pillars of the Kings* can be seen below. A recommended lunch stop is Gibbston Valley Wines, just a little further down the main road on your right.

Return to Queenstown via Lake Hayes to Deer Park Heights. Climbing the hill, you can obtain a magnificent view and visit a number of locations.

Now travel back to Queenstown Airport for your 45-minute Middle-earth Helicopter Explorer Tour with Heliworks. Leaving the airport, you'll climb the steep slopes of the *Misty Mountains* to the *Dimrill Dale* and the *Gates of Khazad-dûm*. The source of the *River Silverlode* lies below and after a pause for photographs you cross towards *Amon Hen*. There are more opportunities for photographs before continuing westward to *Fangorn Forest* and a landing on top of *Dol Baran*, where the vista of *Nan Curunír* (*Isengard* and the *Tower of Orthanc*) unfolds. The great forests beckon and as you fly over the outskirts of *Lothlórien* and *Fangorn* the massive peaks of the *Misty Mountains* tower overhead. *Amon Hen* lies below, where *Lurtz* fought his final battle against *Aragorn*, *Boromir*, *Legolas* and *Gimli*. The return towards Queenstown is via the *Great River*.

> It was an ideal, magical environment for the story, so it was that much easier to get lost in the illusion. I loved being there and I look forward to going back. It's a wonderful place.
>
> VIGGO MORTENSEN

Pierre Vinet

Pierre Vinet

Ian Brodie

Ian Brodie

Above: The Shotover River.

Left: The road goes ever on and on, down from the door where it began.

Overleaf: From Mt Alfred, the Nan Curunír appears with Mt Earnslaw on the right and the forest at Paradise below. In the distant right is the green field where the Fellowship entered Lothlórien. The far alps also appeared in the lighting of the beacons.

Ian Brodie

147

New Line Productions

Above: King Théoden assembled the Rohirrim forces at Dunharrow.

Right: Dunharrow was filmed on private property in the Greenstone Valley. The only way to visit is by horse trek.

Ian Brodie

Mavora Lakes *Fangorn Forest*

A visit to the Mavora Lakes is your passport to a special forested area containing two serene lakes. Their remoteness ensures you are guaranteed solitude with an opportunity to relax and recharge your holiday batteries.

The lakes are situated off the main Five Rivers — Te Anau highway, watch for the signposted road past Mossburn (there is also an access road closer to Te Anau).

From here it is a scenic 39-km, 45-minute drive on an unpaved road to *Fangorn Forest* and *Nen Hithoel*. After travelling 35 km and just prior to the turn off to Mavora Lakes, you'll see a gateway on your right and a repaired fence on your left. On your left is the edge of *Fangorn Forest* so step quietly and you may catch a glimpse of an Ent standing like a sentinel in the trees. It's hard to imagine that during filming over 160 people worked from the paddock on your right.

Climb the fence on your left and walk 250 m in a northwesterly direction. Here *Éomer* and the *Riders of Rohan* burnt the remains of the dead Orcs after their epic battle. The locality is just as you would imagine — a brown hillock with the edge of the deep forest just metres away.

Pierre Vinet

Pierre Vinet

Above top: Gandalf the White with Shadowfax at the edge of Fangorn Forest.

Above: Aragorn, Legolas and Gimli sift through the Orc ashes.

Fangorn Forest was one of the oldest in Middle-earth. A remnant of the Great Forests that covered most of Eriador, it was home to one of the oldest species in Middle-earth — the Ent.

Grown from saplings in the First Age, over the countless years the trees grew to great height and maturity. Some areas of the forest contained deep dells that remained dark and ominous.

ORC MOUND
S45° 19.968'—E168° 10.404'

Mavora Lakes *Nen Hithoel*

Mavora Lakes with the edge of Fangorn Forest.

Accommodation here is limited to a DOC campsite at the south end of the North Mavora, and provides an ideal chance to experience the great New Zealand outdoors. Toilets, barbecues, picnic tables and rubbish collection are provided and water is obtained from the lake. Roads provide easy access to the lake, and New Zealand's benign flora and fauna make for safe camping. Food can be as simple as casting a rod into the lake (the fishing season is 1 October to 30 April) with fat brown trout cruising the food-rich shoreline. A fishing licence is required. For those with plenty of space in the car or campervan don't forget to pack the kayak and mountain bike.

North Mavora became the *Nen Hithoel* (*Sindarin 'Lake of Many Mists'*) foreshore which marked the end of the Fellowship's journey down the *River Anduin*.

As the road passes the south end of North Mavora look for a park bench and a lone toilet. Park here and walk up the slope 150 m into the forest, looking for a large tree stump at the top of the ridge. Here *Merry* and *Pippin* hid from the Orcs, and the large tree shielded *Frodo* from the Uruk-hai. The slopes here were also used to portray *Lurtz* and his band running through the forest to *Nen Hithoel*.

A long oval lake. Nen Hithoel calmed the waters of the Anduin after their rush through the Argonath in preparation for their drop over the Falls of Rauros. After mooring their Elven boats on the western shore they lit a small fire and rested, not realising this day would mark the breaking of the Fellowship.

Go back down to the lakeshore and walk 200 m north, to where the campfire was lit prior to the breaking of the Fellowship. It also marks the spot where *Frodo* and *Sam* were filmed crossing to the eastern shore for their journey to *Mordor*.

Put your hand into the lake and spare a thought for Sean Astin. After each take he changed into dry clothes, warmed himself by a large 'blower' heater and then did it all again.

TREE STUMP: S45° 16.024'—E168° 10.500'
LAKESIDE CAMPFIRE: S45° 15.993'—E168° 10.410'

Mararoa River *Silverlode River*

Ian Brodie

The outlet of the Mararoa River by the swing-bridge at South Mavora was used to portray the junction of the *Silverlode* and *Anduin Rivers* (in the extended DVD) as the Fellowship left *Lothlórien*.

Brown and rainbow trout abound in the river and provide another ready source of food for the barbecue, provided, of course, you've remembered to organise a fishing licence. Because of the tranquillity a population of bush robins reside nearby and New Zealand falcons are often seen soaring in the thermals overhead.

For those not wishing to try a camping lifestyle there are a number of tourist operators based in Queenstown and Te Anau offering 4WD day trips into the area. Queenstown company Heliworks also offer helicopter flights over these locations. The nearby village of Mossburn offers farmstay accommodation and can be used as a base for a day trip into the area. The town of Te Anau is only 45 minutes by car and can also be used as your local touring headquarters.

Tolkien's *Silverlode* was a fair river flowing from its source in *Nanduhirion* through *Lórien* and on into the great *Anduin River*. The pristine beauty of the Mararoa River as it leaves the South Mavora certainly brings his description vividly to mind, in a tranquil and profoundly beautiful location.

Ian Brodie

Above top: South Mavora Lake from the Mararoa River outlet.

Above: View from the campsite at Amon Hen.

Te Anau — an introduction

Ian Brodie

Above: Lake
Te Anau.

Gateway to Fiordland National Park, the township of Te Anau sits beside one of the most splendid lakes in New Zealand. As you stand on the lakefront the brooding bush-covered foothills, draw your eye skywards to towering peaks, and it's easy to understand why this area was chosen to portray the mountainous realms of Middle-earth.

The second largest lake in New Zealand, Lake Te Anau covers 43,200 ha and is over 417 m in depth.

Allow at least three days to fully experience some spectacular journeys including Milford Sound, Doubtful Sound and the Te Ana-au Caves.

Milford Sound is the easiest and most accessible fiord in New Zealand and each year thousands of tourist drive, fly or walk into the area. A popular choice is the fly/drive option, allowing visitors to see the famed Milford Track, Sutherland Falls (one of the worlds highest at 580.3 m) and Sound from the air. After landing at the small airfield a number of cruise options out to the open sea are available. The view from the mouth is stunning, with the return by coach equally impressive, stopping at the Chasm (where the Cleddau River has carved its way through solid rock) and the Homer Tunnel. Also worth a visit is the Wildlife Park, where the rare flightless native bird, the Takahe (*Notornis porphyrio*) can be viewed, along with many others.

A visit to the Redcliff Bar & Café comes highly recommended. During filming in the area, the stars frequented the café and part-owner Megan Harvey has an autographed T-shirt to prove it. One evening dinner coincided with poetry-reading night. After various recitations a deep voice resounded, reciting a Shakespearian sonnet. The reading finished, the visitors applauded and John Rhys Davies took a deep bow and left.

INTERNET
www.fiordland.org.nz

Takaro Road *Fangorn Forest*

A wonderful bush location is situated on Takaro Road. Leaving Te Anau on the main Queenstown highway, turn left onto Kakapo Road just a few kilometres from town. Travel down this road approximately 9 km and turn left onto Takaro Road. After a further 6 km the unsealed road passes through a delightful bushy glade with an unnamed access road on the left.

Park in the little turning area. Filming was undertaken on both sides of the road to portray *Fangorn Forest* with remote cameras strung from high wires to capture *Aragorn* moving through the trees. This lovely forest of red and silver beech seems untouched for millions of years while the forest floor is carpeted with moss of the most intense green.

Beech trees are pollinated by pollen grains caught by the wind. After fertilisation beech flowers produce seeds in the form of small 'nuts'. The seeds rarely blow more than a few metres before falling to the forest floor where they germinate and grow in the shade of the parent tree. The half-light of the forest floor stunts the young seedlings' growth, until a mature tree falls to the ground allowing light to flood in. Once established the trees can grow up to 30 m tall and live for more than 300 years.

Ian Brodie

Above: The edge of Fangorn Forest (Takaro Road).

Overleaf: Early morning at Mavora Lakes.
Ian Brodie

Pierre Vinet

> So it was literally going to another world, a world of clean air, the most crystal-clear water, and the richest of green in the trees. There are these huge, towering summits and volcanoes, and rivers and streams. It's like Tolkien walked across New Zealand and then sat down to write the trilogy.
>
> SEAN ASTIN

FANGORN FOREST
S45° 21.087'—E167° 54.477'

Lake Manapouri and Doubtful Sound

Ian Brodie

Ian Brodie

Above top: Lake Manapouri, looking towards the rough country south of Rivendell.

Above bottom: Pearl Harbour, starting point for the Doubtful Sound excursion.

Situated 12 km from Te Anau, Lake Manapouri (lake of the sorrowing heart) is an area of unspoilt beauty, and the island-studded blue lake and bush-covered Kepler Mountains invite closer exploration.

While filming, unpredictable weather delivered an unseasonable November snowfall. Huge wet snowflakes began to settle on the ground and cover the poor Hobbits. Showing no sign of dissipating, when the snow was over 20 cm deep the cast and crew quickly decided to change scenes to the local Manapouri Hall.

One of the best ways to explore the area is to take the full-day Doubtful Sound excursion with Fiordland Travel. Commencing with a cruise across the lake, the journey continues by bus over the Wilmot Pass (670.9 m) and culminates with a three-hour boat cruise to the sea on Doubtful Sound. Three times longer than Milford Sound and with a surface area ten times larger, Doubtful Sound is home to a resident pod of about 60 bottlenose dolphins and New Zealand fur seals can be seen basking on the rocks at the Nee Islets. Scattered around the sound is the rare and very shy Fiordland crested penguin.

Over millions of years the collision of rock and ice has sculpted this landscape, now cloaked in dense cool temperate rainforest. The 'sound of silence' and complete isolation as one cruises the sound is one of its many charms.

On the journey across Lake Manapouri cast your eyes upwards to the high mountaintops on your right, by Freeman Burn. Situated far up in these alpine peaks are the Norwest Lakes — locations used to show the Fellowship heading south from *Rivendell*.

Norwest Lakes
south of Rivendell/flight to the ford

Ian Brodie

The helicopter is no stranger to this part of the world; in the 1960s it became the 'mount' for commercial deer hunters, who combed the area for prize venison. Commercial hunting gave way to farming but the helicopter remains and now serves as the perfect transportation for reaching the more remote locations.

As the ring heads south a wild and rugged land opens in front of the Fellowship and perched high in the Kepler Mountains, the Norwest Lakes are closely reminiscent of Middle-earth.

The opening sequence of the *Flight to the Ford* showing *Arwen* and *Frodo* in the desperate escape from the *Black Riders* was also filmed near Te Anau. The location is only accessible on the longer Heliworks' helicopter tour.

Aerial view of the area used to film Arwen's flight.

Ian Brodie

Previous and above:
Norwest Lakes are a
remote and beautiful
location.

Ian Brodie

Right: Norwest
Lakes on a perfect
autumn day.

Ian Brodie

Ian Brodie

Ian Brodie

Above: The area used to show the Fellowship heading south, through Eregion.

Left: A Heliworks Squirrel helicopter perched in the remote Norwest Lakes area.

Central Otago — an introduction

Pierre Vinet

Ian Brodie

Above top: Orcs on the rampage in Rohan.

Above: A rebuilt Chinese miner's cottage near Poolburn.

The cycle of the seasons are more apparent in Central Otago than anywhere else in New Zealand. In summer temperatures exceed 30°C and the hills shimmer in the burning heat; in winter temperatures as low as –15°C cover the trees in ghostly white hoar frost. In autumn the region becomes a sea of gold as poplars and willows prepare for winter; in spring fruit trees welcome the warmer weather with a stunning blossom display.

The lure of gold in 1862 brought people to the region. As the easily won gold was soon depleted the population decreased, until the 1890s, when the idea of dredging for gold saw a resurgence in the population of nearby Alexandra.

When the dredging began to dwindle, residents discovered the soil was rich in potash and phosphoric acid and fruit orchards became the new gold.

The township of Clyde still has a number of original buildings from the 1800s, serving wonderful food incorporating the best in local produce.

Alexandra is the main service town for the Central Otago Region and has a number of attractions related to the gold discoveries. Very popular in summer, it has the distinction of the lowest rainfall of any town in New Zealand.

A great way to explore this region is via the Central Otago Rail Trail. Although the trains have now gone, 150 km of track from Clyde to Middlemarch has been converted into a trail for bikes, horses or pedestrians. While easily accessible from the road for a day trip, to really savour the spectacular scenery, consider hiring a cycle and stopping overnight at one of the small country hotels en-route.

Ian Brodie

Ian Brodie

The stark schist stacked rocks of the Poolburn area provided a rugged backdrop for the Orcs to scurry through en route to Isengard.

INTERNET
www.tco.org.nz

Poolburn *Rohan*

Poolburn Dam was completed in 1931, as a storage lake to irrigate the Ida Valley below. The land is rich and during the height of the gold rush there were five hotels dispensing liquid warmth to miners toiling in the harsh environment. Today it's a popular recreational area and the reservoir is richly stocked with brown trout.

On reaching the lake, there is an excellent view across to the location of the small village where *Morwen* sent her children to safety before attack. No trace of the village remains but the area is immediately recognisable.

A number of other sites were used in this locality to show the Hobbits being rushed to *Saruman* and the epic chase by *Aragorn*, *Gimli* and *Legolas*.

Above: Poolburn's fishing huts were camouflaged as farmhouses.

Right: The Orcs' plundering of the small Rohirrim village would be avenged at the Battle of Helm's Deep.

VIEWPOINT OF *ROHIRRIM* VILLAGE:
S45° 17.769'—E169° 44.346'

LOCATION OF POOLBURN UNIT BASE:
S45° 17.610'—E 169°43.623'

Ida Valley *Rohan*

The area surrounding the Poolburn Reservoir high on the Rough Ridge Range in the Ida Valley was used extensively to portray *Rohan*. It was the perfect choice, as the rolling hills with distinctive rocky tors and expansive vistas invite comparison with the realm of the *Riddermark*.

Poolburn Reservoir is remote and the rough road from the valley floor is recommended for four-wheel-drive vehicles only. It is also very exposed and care should be taken; the weather can change quickly with snow possible during three seasons.

Situated an impressive 40-minute drive from Alexandra, the sealed drive to the foot of the ranges takes you to the village of Omakau, where the nearby racecourse was used as the production office. Take a right turn into the small hamlet of Ophir. Gold was discovered in 1863, and Ophir was named after the biblical realm where the Queen of Sheba obtained gold for King Solomon.

The road now climbs across the Raggedy Range, with wonderful views from the summit of a land seemingly untouched by humans. The sky is usually an intense blue and in summer the shimmering heat haze seems to distort distances into a golden sphere. After descending to the valley floor turn right at the Poolburn Hotel onto Moa Creek Road and continue on to Webster Lane, where you need to turn left into the unpaved road.

The climb to Poolburn itself commences beside Bonspiel Station, and for those without appropriate vehicles, it is a logical stopping space. The local landowners organise tours of Poolburn in their 4WD and as many of the locations were situated on their property they are the ideal hosts to take you to *Rohan*. They also have home-stay accommodation available in original Chinese miners' huts.

Pierre Vinet

The green and rolling hills of Rohan were gifted to the Rohirrim by Cirion of Gondor in TA2510.

The cast and crew spent many weeks filming at Poolburn, staying at a number of localities including Alexandra and Cromwell. Due to the condition of the access road they met at the foot of the hill and were transported up by 4WD. This resulted in very long days, often starting at 5 a.m. and finishing at 8 p.m.

Waiau River and Kepler Track
River Anduin

Ian Brodie

Waiau River from a
viewpoint near the
Kepler Track.

Flowing from Lake Te Anau to Lake Manapouri, the Waiau River was used to portray parts of the majestic *River Anduin*. Bush-clad banks perfectly set the scene illustrating the first part of the river journey undertaken by the Fellowship before they reached the *Brown Lands*, the desolate and treeless area between *Mirkwood* and the *Emyn Muil*, where long ago the *Ent Wives* made their gardens. Sections of the river are accessible from the main Te Anau – Manapouri road and the entire waterway can be viewed on the longer of the three different Heliworks' helicopter tour options from Queenstown. Luxmore Jet also operates boat tours along the river.

A more energetic option for the hale and hearty is to undertake the 67-km Kepler Track, commencing in Te Anau. A reasonable level of fitness is required to complete the full tramp over three to four days, which traverses lake edges, beech forests, mountaintops and a U-shaped glacial valley, and provides a more personal appreciation of our heroes' journey!

For those with less time take the main Te Anau / Manapouri highway and turn right at the DOC Rainbow Reach sign. As the unsealed road first veers left (and before it veers right again) turn right down the unmarked track. A magnificent view of the *River Anduin* can be obtained from this viewpoint. If you continue a further 2 km down the access road there is a swing bridge across the river and the opportunity to take a shorter walk on the Kepler Track. The journey is 10.9 km one way but even a short stroll will take you into the native beech forest and provide beautiful views of the river. More information on the Kepler Track can be obtained from the local DOC Headquarters in Te Anau.

Pierre Vinet

> Tolkien was writing about a different world, a different land, a primitive land and a primitive time in history. New Zealand — breathtakingly beautiful — is just perfect for that.
>
> JOHN RHYS-DAVIES

RIVER ANDUIN VIEWPOINT
S45° 29.755'—E167° 40.159'

A New Zealand tour

For a voyage of discovery through Middle-earth Aotearoa the following twenty-three-day itinerary includes most of the important locations. The tour starts in Auckland and ends in Christchurch allowing for convenient connections with Air New Zealand – The Official Airline to Middle-earth.

DAY ONE: Auckland – Matamata – Taupo
  ▷ *Hobbiton*

DAY TWO: Taupo – The Chateau

DAY THREE: The Chateau
  ▷ *Mordor*

DAY FOUR: The Chateau – Ohakune
  ▷ *Ithilien and Mordor*

DAY FIVE: Ohakune – Otaki
  ▷ *River Anduin*

DAY SIX: Otaki – Wellington
  ▷ *Leaving the Shire*
  ▷ *Pelennor Fields*

DAY SEVEN: Wellington
  ▷ *Leaving the Shire*
  ▷ *Embassy Theatre*
  ▷ *Chocolate Fish Café*
  ▷ *Dunharrow*

Pierre Vinet

Everything here is more magnificent. The landscape is familiar in the sense it's been formed by rain — just as Tolkien's Oxfordshire was — but the vegetation is unusual and the mountains seem so much sharper. If you're looking for what the poets used to call 'the awful' — a sense of awe — that is what you find in New Zealand. And it's wild in a way that England isn't wild.

IAN MCKELLEN

INTERNET
www.newzealand.com
www.conservation.govt.nz
www.airnewzealand.com

Pierre Vinet

DAY EIGHT: Wellington – Martinborough
- ▷ *River Anduin*
- ▷ *Rivendell*
- ▷ *Isengard Gardens*

DAY NINE: Martinborough
- ▷ *Dimholt Road*

DAY TEN: Martinborough – Wellington – Nelson
- ▷ *Artisans*

DAY ELEVEN: Nelson
- ▷ *Chetwood Forest*
- ▷ *Rough Country South of Rivendell*
- ▷ *Dimrill Dale*

DAY TWELVE: Nelson – Methven

DAY THIRTEEN: Methven – Twizel
- ▷ *Edoras*
- ▷ *Pelennor Fields*

DAY FOURTEEN: Twizel – Wanaka
- ▷ *Flight to the Ford*
- ▷ *Rough Country South of Rivendell*

DAY FIFTEEN: Wanaka – Glenorchy
- ▷ *Pillars of the Argonath*
- ▷ *Ford of Bruinen*
- ▷ *Gladden Fields*
- ▷ *Amon Hen*
- ▷ *Ithilien Camp*

We did everything – bungy jumping,
surfing, motorcycle riding, we did it all.
Sightseeing, taking in the America's Cup
regatta – we were the Fellowship around
town in New Zealand.

SEAN ASTIN

DAY SIXTEEN: Glenorchy – Queenstown
  ▷ *Isengard*
  ▷ *Lothlórien*
  ▷ *Amon Hen*

DAY SEVENTEEN: Queenstown
  ▷ *Deer Park Heights*
  ▷ *Dimrill Dale*

DAY EIGHTEEN: Queenstown – Mavora Lakes – Te Anau
  ▷ *Amon Hen*
  ▷ *Fangorn Forest*

DAY NINETEEN: Te Anau
  ▷ *River Anduin*

DAY TWENTY: Te Anau – Queenstown

DAY TWENTY ONE: Queenstown – Franz Josef

DAY TWENTY TWO: Franz Josef
  ▷ *Lighting of the Beacon*

DAY TWENTY THREE: Franz Josef – Christchurch

The woods were nearby. A beautiful river was always nearby. No matter how urban a place was, it was never very far away from something that felt more or less primeval.

VIGGO MORTENSEN

INTERNET
www.camping.co.nz

Index

NAMÁRIË

New Line Productions